THE ETHICS AND POLITICS OF HUMANITARIAN INTERVENTION

Notre Dame Studies on International Peace
Joan B. Kroc Institute for International Peace Studies
University of Notre Dame

With the end of the Cold War the promise and relevance of peace research have significantly increased. The issues now addressed include the nature of the world order, international institutions, the resolution of deadly conflicts, humanitarian security, and ethical issues raised by violence, environmental degradation, and poverty. Peace studies probe these problems and search for comprehensive solutions.

Notre Dame Studies on International Peace focuses on these vital issues. Scholarly perspectives are combined with sound policy recommendations and the setting of normative standards. The books published here emanate primarily from the research work of the Kroc Institute and its other activities, especially the annual Theodore M. Hesburgh, C.S.C., Lectures on Ethics and Public Policy.

These lectures were launched in 1995 by the Joan B. Kroc Institute for International Peace Studies to honor the lifetime commitment of the President Emeritus of the University of Notre Dame to the promotion of ethical values in public policy and his continuing support of the Institute. *The Ethics and Politics of Humanitarian Intervention* results from the first lectures in 1995 delivered by Professor Stanley Hoffmann of Harvard University.

Previously published in the series *Notre Dame Studies on International Peace* is *India and the Bomb: Public Opinion and Nuclear Options,* edited by David Cortright and Amitabh Mattoo.

Joan B. Kroc Institute for International Peace Studies was established at the University of Notre Dame in 1986. In addition to research projects, the Institute has an international graduate program and an undergraduate concentration in peace studies. It is a premier institute in its field in the United States. More information can be obtained from the Kroc Institute, P.O. Box 639, University of Notre Dame, Notre Dame, IN 46556, USA (phone 219-631-6970, fax 219-631-6973).

THE ETHICS
AND POLITICS
OF
HUMANITARIAN
INTERVENTION

Stanley Hoffmann

With contributions by Robert C. Johansen, James P. Sterba, and Raimo Väyrynen

University of Notre Dame Press

Notre Dame, Indiana

Library of Congress Cataloging-in-Publication Data
Hoffmann, Stanley.
    The ethics and politics of humanitarian intervention / Stanley
Hoffmann ; with contributions by Robert C. Johansen, James P. Sterba,
and Raimo Väyrynen.
        p.   cm. — (Theodore M. Hesburgh lectures on ethics and public
policy ; v. 1)
    Includes bibliographical references and index.
    ISBN 0-268-00935-X (alk. paper). — ISBN 0-268-00936-8 (alk.
paper)
    1. Intervention (International law)—Moral and ethical aspects.
2. War victims—Bosnia and Hercegovina.   3. Yugoslav War, 1991—
Bosnia and Hercegovina.   I. Johansen, Robert C.   II. Sterba, James
P.   III. Väyrynen, Raimo.   IV. Title.   V. Series.
JX4481.H63   1997
341.5'84'0949709049—dc20   96-28968
                                                                      CIP

The paper used in this publication meets the minimum requirements
of the American National Standard for Information
Sciences—Permanence of Paper for Printed Library Materials, ANSI
Z39.48-9184.

CONTENTS

CONTRIBUTORS

Stanley Hoffmann is the C. Douglas Dillon Professor of the Civilization of France at Harvard University and Chairman of the Minda de Gunzburg Center for European Studies. He has authored several books on ethics, international theory, world order, and European and French issues. Most recently he has authored *Janus and Minerva* (1986) and *The European Sisyphus: Essays on Europe* (1995) and coauthored *The New European Community* (1991) and *After the Cold War* (1993).

Robert C. Johansen is Professor of Government and International Studies at the University of Notre Dame and the Director of Graduate Studies at its Joan B. Kroc Institute for International Peace Studies. His main research interests are in the study of world order and international institutions. Among many other publications he has coauthored *The Constitutional Foundations of World Peace* (1993).

James P. Sterba is Professor of Philosophy and Fellow of the Joan B. Kroc Institute for International Peace Studies at the University of Notre Dame. He has authored and edited several books on ethical issues pertaining to the use of force, feminism, and environment, most recently *Contemporary Social and Political Philosophy* (1995) and *Morality in Practice* (1996).

Raimo Väyrynen is Professor of Government and International Studies and John M. Regan, Jr. Director of the Joan B. Kroc Institute for International Peace Studies at the University of Notre Dame. His research interests are in conflict and security studies, and theory and history of international relations. His most recent books are *Military Industrialization and Economic Development* (1992) and a biography of Urho Kekkonen (1994).

1

INTRODUCTION
How Much Force in Humanitarian Intervention?
Raimo Väyrynen

THE EVENTS IN the former Yugoslavia have been an acid test both for international principles of peace and sovereignty and international practices in peacekeeping and humanitarian intervention. With the peace process underway, it is important to consider the lessons of Yugoslavia's breakup and develop guidelines by which peace in the region can be stabilized, human rights respected, and economies developed. In fact, the Yugoslavian case provides a benchmark by which the efforts to prevent escalation of future international crises and the viability of multi-ethnic federal states should be assessed.

1. Sovereignty and War

With regard to territorial sovereignty, the former Yugoslavia has experienced a sea change; out of a sovereign federal state five independent states have emerged. Their international position and internal cohesion, however, remains precarious and their mutual relations have barely been institutionalized. Yet there is no alternative to a nation-state model in the former Yugoslavia; proposals to reassemble the now independent states into a loose, confederal arrangement are utterly unrealistic.[1] In fact, the former Yugoslavia needs a full but benign implementation of the principle of sovereignty both within and between the new political entities.

This guideline presupposes that the newly independent states have a generally recognized territorial base on which there is no disagreement with other states. Territory and nationalism are intertwined, and their relationship may even assume rather perverse forms when, for example, landscapes are idealized and linked with historical memories. On the other hand, a consolidated territory provides a basis for a status quo and hence for political stability. Especially in ethnically divided societies, it is far better if national feelings are grounded in common territory than in claims of ethnic superiority.[2]

Internally strong and resilient states are an important precondition for peace and stability. Weak states, especially ones facing the risk of collapse, are synonymous with internal wars and external involvements in them.[3] To avoid a situation in which the weakness of states threatens peace and stability in the Balkans, the internal reconstruction of the states in the region should have a high priority. This would require both the rebuilding of the industrial and transportation infrastructures and the institutionalization of and respect for democracy, human and minority rights, and ethnic reconciliation. These objectives would be well served by the strengthening of democracy, especially in Croatia and Serbia, in both of which it is inadequate at best.

As of spring 1996, the former Yugoslavia has inched towards a stable territorial demarcation in which frontiers are either assured by international treaties or are otherwise uncontested. The main problems concern the position of the Albanian population in Kosovo and Macedonia and its territorial implications, the role of Montenegro as a part of Serbia, and, of course, the future of Bosnia as a unified state. Political stability in the former Yugoslavia also presupposes that the Erdun agreement on the status of Eastern Slavonia is respected and implemented and thereby, Croatia regains its original territorial basis.

A major reason for the resort to military force in the former Yugoslavia was the single-minded focus of Western political leaders on administrative, republican borders. Commitment to preserving existing borders was intended to stave off the plans for a Greater Croatia and Greater Serbia, which would have required carving up Croatia and Bosnia. Acceptance of the existing borders also eliminated the risk of endless territorial disputes among the new political entities. Against this backdrop it was assumed that a new basis for stability would be achieved by creating sovereign states from the former republics of the Federal Republic of Yugoslavia. This approach satisfied nationalist leaders in the republics, except that Croatia and Serbia were unwilling to approve the sovereignty of Bosnia and Herzegovina.

It turned out that the sovereignty principle was incompatible with another organizing idea, viz. the national self-determination. It was also inconsistent with the OSCE (Organization for Security and Cooperation in Europe) principle permitting the change of borders only by peaceful means, which spoke for retaining Yugoslavia as a unified state. The application of the principle of national self-determination would have permitted the Croatian Serbs either to join Serbia or have a sufficient degree of autonomy. It would also have meant the incorporation of Bosnian Serbs and Croats into their respective mother countries, resulting thus in the division of Bosnia. Had this price been considered acceptable, a greater flexibility in drawing borders might have opened up new chances for a mutually acceptable political and territorial compromise.[4] The experiences with various cantonization plans in 1992–94 suggest that even though such plans were unable to stop the war, they catalyzed new developments which ultimately paved the way to a compromise.[5]

Flexibility with regard to the sovereignty principle was not encouraged by the international community. The new sovereign states in the former Yugoslavia had to be created by war, which started in Croatia in June 1991 and in Bosnia in April 1992. The international community condemned the use of military force and argued that the gains made by war would not be recognized. However, the community did not offer ingredients for a compromise solution that would have given the nationalist leaders of the republics reasons to end the fighting. Instead, incompatible visions of Croatian and Serbian nationalists persisted, and hence "there was no negotiation to speak of; no give-and-take; no progress." The result was the "conversation of the deaf" and the increasing reliance on military force as an instrument of politics.[6] Thus, the stress on sovereignty contributed to war.

In spite of several efforts, no negotiated solution for an early end to the occupations and wars in Croatia and Bosnia could be reached.

In Bosnia the fighting continued for three and a half years before the Dayton accord established a more lasting cease-fire and demarcated the territorial spheres of control for the Bosnian Serbs and the Croat-Muslim federation. During the war the international community did not remain completely passive. It tried to limit the extent and damage of fighting and safeguard the delivery of humanitarian aid to the civilian population in Sarajevo and elsewhere suffering from the war. While the international community failed to prevent and stop the fighting by diplomatic means, the question remains whether it was more successful in protecting humanitarian values during the course of war.

2. Coercive Instruments

In the early phases of the Yugoslavian crisis, the international community held a strong belief that a proper combination of diplomatic and economic measures would defuse it. Until June 1991 the European Community (EC) "negotiated with few instruments of coercion,"[7] but sensing the ineffectiveness of this approach, it shifted from economic rewards to punishments. By August 1991 the EC realized that even economic punishments were inadequate to cope with the volatile situation, and coercive backup was needed for diplomatic efforts. This conclusion gave rise to the idea of a European "interposition force" to separate the fighting parties and keep peace in Yugoslavia. The lack of political agreement among major powers and the inadequate European command and logistical capabilities led, however, to the rejection of the force by the EC in September 1991.

The failure of the EC to send troops to Yugoslavia to keep peace made the involvement of the United Nations (UN) necessary. In December 1991 the UN Security Council decided to send ten thousand troops to Yugoslavia to prevent the fighting in Croatia from continuing. In hindsight, the UN Protection Force (UNPROFOR) was by most standards a failure. While it occasionally helped to stabilize the local situation and assure the delivery of humanitarian aid, it failed in the bigger task of contributing to a long-term solution to the Yugoslavian crisis.

The reasons for the failure were more political than military. The political agreement negotiated by Cyrus Vance, the UN representative, did not address the border issues which created a time bomb, especially in Croatia. Serbia had agreed to the deployment of UNPROFOR along the battlelines in Krajina and Eastern and Western Slavonia, hoping to freeze its territorial gains. In reality, a bomb was ticking as Croatia started acquiring more weapons to prepare itself for the military return of the occupied territories. Military operations were carried out in Western Slavonia and Krajina in May and August 1995, respectively. The UN had no way, nor any real reason, to defend these territories against the Croatian attack. Both in Croatia and Bosnia, UNPROFOR's mandate was unrealistic; it contained ambitious political goals without giving the forces adequate instruments and political support to pursue them.[8]

When the war was kindled in Bosnia, the UN did not start a separate operation but rather expanded UNPROFOR's mandate as a "makeshift solution" in which the role of NATO was prominent.[9] UNPROFOR had the task of supporting the humanitarian operations of the UN High Commissioner for Refugees (UNHCR), for instance, by keeping the Sarajevo airport open and even delivering relief; conducting peacekeeping operations to support the six UN Protected Areas (UNPA) in Bosnia; and directing the preventive military deployment in Macedonia. In contrast to these ambitious mandates, UNPROFOR's military resources and rules of engagement seriously limited its operational capabilities.

3. Lessons of Yugoslavia

The assessment of the EC and UN operations in Yugoslavia obviously depends on the criteria used. If the standards are rather modest, the conclusion can be fairly positive. The UN was able to deliver humanitarian assistance in Bosnia in difficult conditions. It had some successes in its "field diplomacy" which resulted, for example, in local anti-sniping and harvesting agreements, exchange of bodies and prisoners, and family reunifications.[10] It can even be argued that for more than three years, UNPROFOR was able to prevent the resumption of fighting in Croatia. Thus, given the constraints of the situation, UNPROFOR was able to provide some tangible help to the civilian populations.

Concerning the European Community, it can be argued, as Hans-Dietrich Genscher has done, that its political mediation and preventive diplomatic recognition of Slovenia and Croatia were successful, since they stopped the fighting in these countries with the Yugoslav National Army (JNA).[11] Such an interpretation, however, overlooks the fact that the EC policy towards Croatia encouraged rather than prevented its use of military force in Bosnia and also gave a good pretext for the Serbs to become militarily involved in the conflict. Moreover, fighting in Croatia had been discontinued before the recognition in January 1992.

Applying more stringent criteria, an inescapable conclusion from the Yugoslavian crisis is that a diplomatic strategy of conflict prevention must either go an extra mile to develop creative political solutions or be ready to back up mediation by the threat or use of coercive power. Sometimes economic sanctions may be enough, but in most cases, even if consistently and effectively implemented, they do not make a significant difference to the outcome. There must be readiness to use force in an early phase of the conflict to convince the parties that major powers are serious in their policies. The resort to coercive actions does not, of course, require a massive use of firepower. There are less drastic military measures to communicate determination and commitment.[12]

The emphasis on the need to be prepared to use force to achieve political ends in an intractable conflict can, of course, be criticized on a number of counts. A practical counterargument is that major powers—possessing necessary hardware, logistical, and command capabilities—are unwilling to take political risks embedded in military operations, especially ground operations. They fear the escalation of conflict and entrapment in it, for instance due to difficulty of the local terrain or the intransigence of warlords, leading to casualties and burgeoning political costs.[13] If major powers are unwilling to share the burden and carry out operations, the chances of success are, according to this reasoning, limited. An alternative view advocates that small and medium-sized countries assume a more active role in innovative forms of peacekeeping, but very few of them appear to be ready for it.

The moral argument rejects the passivity of the international community if people are killed or otherwise suffer massively. The international community has to become involved sooner or later, as the Rwandan case shows, and it is more cost-effective by humanitarian, political, and economic criteria to intervene early rather than late. A major problem is that, caught between reasons to act and fear of the risks, governments tend to initiate halfhearted measures, such as economic sanctions or humanitarian operations without sufficient political commitment to pursue them seriously.

The half-measures easily result in internally inconsistent policies whose success is at the mercy of the strongest parties to the conflict. Peacekeepers can be harassed, taken hostage, and even killed if they lack adequate resources or the right to respond under the rules of engagement. It is conventional wisdom that in Somalia and Bosnia the goals of the humanitarian and military operations were not clearly defined, and their implementation became so closely intertwined that both ultimately suffered. The Deputy Force Commander of UNPROFOR points out that the inclusion of the humanitarian element in its military mandate "dangerously linked" it to the ongoing conflict and jeopardized its impartiality, or, alternatively, created an impression that the humanitarian aid could be "punched through" by the use of force.[14]

In traditional peacekeeping, consent of the parties and impartiality of operations are the main foundations of success. Consent, however, requires a cease-fire agreement, which cannot always be negotiated. In the absence of such an agreement, an orthodox peacekeeping operation cannot be started and humanitarian operations, if any, must be carried out in an evenhanded manner without military protection. Several non-governmental organizations, the International Committee of the Red Cross included, in fact prefer such an approach; victims of emergencies have to be helped without any regard to their ethnic, religious, or other affiliations. Charity should be based only on humanitarian motives and is politically blind.

4. A Humanitarian Emphasis

Experiences in Afghanistan, Bosnia, Liberia, and in particular, Somalia show that the local powerholders can obstruct the delivery of humanitarian aid and unduly benefit by confiscating it. Therefore, the ability to meet the humanitarian criteria requires at least some armed protection of the convoys and deliveries. If the United Nations operates only under the mandate of Chapter VI of its Charter and if complete impartiality is the aim, then the local power relations must be accepted and the humanitarian access must be negotiated on their basis. Such an approach will probably lead to untenable situations in which aid workers and peacekeepers become mere marionettes in local power politics.

To avoid this dilemma, peacekeepers must have the right to use limited force to protect the deliveries and show determination for deterrent purposes. "When this happens, force should be applied in the necessary measure, but for a limited time, returning to negotiations as soon as the conditions posed are met by the counterpart."[15] This advice is in many respects sound. It sends the message that the use of force by international troops is limited to humanitarian purposes and self-defense, thus avoiding the escalation of the conflict. The message is that if the adversaries permit international operations to protect the victims, they will not be challenged by peacekeepers in a more serious way.

This position has, however, several drawbacks. For instance, it does not entitle the international contingents to use force even if they observe war crimes and blatant violations of human rights. One solution to this dilemma is to stress the support peacekeeping can give to protect human rights. This requires "increased emphasis on international legal instruments," including laws on human rights, refugees, and warfare. Peacekeepers must be trained to monitor, if not enforce, the observance of these laws.[16]

The problem in the humanitarian emphasis in peacekeeping is that it may require a greater commitment to military action than the UN and its member states are ready to accept. Even if their approval exists—and the recent experience of the International Enforcement Force (IFOR) in Bosnia creates doubts in this regard—

the efforts to prevent war crimes and human rights violations do not necessarily stop the fighting. In such a situation the major powers must decide whether they are ready to initiate a large-scale peace enforcement operation as the only way to stop killings. It happened against Iraq in 1991, but since then, cautiousness has become a hallmark of enforcement operations. It seems that the very complexity of current crises deters third parties from serious involvement because its consequences are unpredictable.

Perhaps there is a threshold which must be passed before the international community overcomes the constraints created by the fears of casualties and of entrapment. Such a threshold was obviously passed in Bosnia in August 1995, when information spread on the Serbian takeover of Srebrenica and the killing of thousands of Muslims. In retaliation, NATO started bombing Serbian sites of heavy weapons. Even then the policy minimized risks, because a third party's use of airpower cannot drag it into a protracted conflict as easily as reliance on ground forces.

The NATO bombings were criticized by many, but the conclusion seems inescapable that they broke the political logjam. The military operations of NATO and the French and U.S. diplomatic initiatives, utilizing the political space created by the Croatian military recovery of its territories, paved the way to the Dayton accord and consequently, the peace process in Bosnia. This is not to say that an extensive use of military force is necessarily conducive to peace, but it does say that there are situations in which diplomatic and even economic measures are inadequate to restructure the political situation. If forceful measures can change the course towards a negotiated solution, a limited, politically informed use of military force can be defended on purely humanitarian grounds.

NOTES

1. Such a proposal has been made, for example, by Flora Lewis, "Reassembling Yugoslavia," *Foreign Policy* 98 (1995): 132–44.

2. These problems are further discussed in Raimo Väyrynen, "Terri-

tory, Nation States and Nationalism," in *The Future of Nation States in Europe,* ed. Jyrki Iivonen (Aldershot: Edward Elgar, 1993), 159–78.

3. This argument is further developed by K. J. Holsti, "War, Peace, and the State of State," *International Political Science Review* 16, no. 4 (1995): 319–39.

4. For an incisive analysis on political and territorial contradictions in the division of Yugoslavia, see Susan Woodward, *Balkan Tragedy: Chaos and Dissolution after the Cold War* (Washington, D.C.: Brookings Institution, 1995), 199–222.

5. Håkan Wiberg, "Making Peace in the Former Yugoslavia: Problems and Lessons," in *The Search for Peace in the Mediterranean Region: Problems and Prospects,* ed. James Calleja, Håkan Wiberg, and Salvino Busuttil (Msida, Malta: Mireva, 1994), 243–49.

6. Laura Silber and Allan Little, *Yugoslavia: Death of a Nation* (New York: Penguin, 1996), 147–53.

7. James E. Goodby, "Conflict in Europe: The Case of Yugoslavia," in *Regional Conflicts: The Challenge to US-Russian Co-operation,* ed. James E. Goodby (New York: Oxford University Press, 1995), 163–64.

8. The best analysis of the UN failure in Yugoslavia is still Rosalynn Higgins, "The New United Nations and Former Yugoslavia," *International Affairs* 69, no. 3 (1993): 165–83. See also Åge Eknes, "The United Nations' Predicament in the Former Yugoslavia," in *The United Nations and Civil Wars,* ed. Thomas G. Weiss (Boulder, Colo.: Lynne Rienner, 1995), 109–26.

9. The term comes from Victor-Yves Ghebali, "UNPROFOR in the Former Yugoslavia: The Misuse of Peacekeeping and Associated Conflict Management Techniques," in *New Dimensions of Peacekeeping,* ed. Daniel Warner (Dordrecht: Martinus Nijhoff, 1995), 18–20.

10. Graham Day, "Missed Opportunities in the Balkans? Lessons for Peacemaking and Preventive Diplomacy from the Former Yugoslavia," in *Peacemaking and Preventive Diplomacy in the New World (Dis)order,* ed. David R. Black and Susan J. Rolston (Halifax, Nova Scotia: Center for Foreign Policy Studies, Dalhousie University, 1995), 85–87.

11. Hans-Dietrich Genscher, *Errinnerungen* (Berlin: Siedler Verlag, 1995), 693–94.

12. A nuanced approach to the use of coercive power is developed in Alexander George, *Forceful Persuasion: Coercive Diplomacy as an Alternative to War* (Washington, D.C.: The United States Institute of Peace, 1991).

13. The critical case is outlined, for example, in Enrico Augelli and Craig N. Murphy, "Lessons of Somalia for Future Multilateral Humanitarian Assistance Operations," *Global Governance* 1, no. 3 (1995): 342–45.

14. J. A. MacInnis, "Enhancing UN Response: Lessons from

UNPROFOR," in *UN Rapid Reaction Capabilities: Requirements and Prospects*, ed. David Cox and Albert Legault (Clemensport, Nova Scotia: The Canadian Peacekeeping Press, 1995), 121–23.
    15. Augelli and Murphy, "Lessons of Somalia," 348–50.
    16. MacInnis, "Enhancing UN Response," 125–26.

2

SOVEREIGNTY AND THE ETHICS OF INTERVENTION

Stanley Hoffmann

THE TRADITIONAL LEGAL order of international relations—whether or not it actually began with the treaties of Westphalia—has had as its cornerstone the principle of state sovereignty. It is a tricky concept, and the most serviceable definition is Hedley Bull's, who, in *The Anarchical Society*, describes sovereignty as independence from any outside authority. The corollaries of this principle are the norm of the equality of rights of states and the norm of nonintervention in a state's domestic affairs (another name for this is the duty to respect a state's domestic jurisdiction). This set of norms was enshrined in the Charter of the UN. To be sure, the Charter mentions human rights among the purposes of the organized international community, but it also reasserts the principle of state sovereignty and the principle of consent, except in enforcement actions ordered by the Security Council under Chapter VII.

The norm of nonintervention, as analyzed by Lori Damrosch,[1] has two main functions. The first is to minimize inter-state conflict. Sovereignty is, so to speak, the actors' side of a coin of which the collective side is anarchy—the absence, by definition, of any power superior to the states. Sovereignty can all too easily lead to conflict—and indeed the resort to war was considered a right of states until the limitations introduced by the Covenant of the League and extended by the Charter of the UN. If states clashed not only over the usual range of conflicting interests but also because of interventions in each other's domestic affairs, anarchy could become unmanageable. A second function is the preservation of a state's autonomy, "but what is fundamentally at stake is the realization of the human rights of the individuals who live within state boundaries."[2] If one believes that the rights of states are ultimately derived from the rights of those individuals, one can see that the principle of state sovereignty has a human rights component: individuals have the right to live in a state of their choice, or (at least) to whose rule they assent, a right that is not to be violated by outsiders. Thus, the norm of nonintervention is essential both to the Realist theory of international relations and to Michael Walzer's "legalist paradigm."[3] Realism describes the international system as a network of state interactions in a condition of anarchy, and, normatively, it recommends a moderate definition of the national interest as likely to lead to the most bearable kind of anarchy; such a moderate definition would limit interventions in domestic affairs, especially forcible ones, as much as possible. As for the legalist paradigm, it leads to an ethic of states rights which is a mix of two different liberalisms: an individualistic one, which bases states' rights on the rights of individuals, and a communitarian one, in which states are seen as political communities, assimilated to individuals with rights, and enjoying their rights as long as there is a "presumption of fit" between the individual members and the state; even if the government is nondemocratic, but as long as the state is founded on the principle of self-determination, i.e., it is a national state, foreign interventions are to be ruled out: the community's autonomy requires freedom from outside intervention.

The system of perfectly sovereign states was always something of an ideal-type: in reality, many states were subjugated or controlled by others, or had limitations on their internal sovereignty imposed on them. But the contemporary challenge to sovereignty is much more profound. As most commentators on international relations have observed, there is a growing discrepancy between the norms of sovereignty and the traditional legal organization of the international system on the one hand, and the realities of a world in which the distinction between domestic politics and international politics is crumbling. The ideology of sovereignty seemed at first to have been reenforced by decolonization; the kind of self-determination that was encouraged by the UN in the cases of colonial possessions[4] focused not on ethnic groups but on territories, and thus respected the borders traced by the colonial powers (cf. the treatment of Katanga's secession by the UN during the Congo crisis). This led to a vast increase in the number of sovereign states. But even then, sovereignty was being affected by a number of long-term trends.

The most familiar is economic interdependence, a phenomenon which is both a condition and a construct. Whatever their attempts at insulation, most states are deeply marked by events and decisions that originate outside their borders: in the realm of economic policies (trade, debt, interest rates, etc.), in environmental issues (pollution, ozone depletion, acid rain, depletion of fish stocks, global warming, etc.), and with respect to refugees seeking asylum and to migrations. Hence there is an increasing discrepancy between legal sovereignty and what Robert Keohane has called operational sovereignty,[5] i.e., the amount of autonomy that a state can actually enjoy or the amount of competences actually at its disposal. This trend was reenforced by the establishment of international institutions whose role it is to constrain that operational sovereignty, or whose rules of decision mark the passage from sovereignty-as-independence to pooled sovereignty: GATT, the European Monetary System, environmental institutions, the IMF, the new World Trade Organization, etc.

A second trend lasted throughout the cold war period, and was actually initiated by the new ideological powers of the interwar period: the ideological wars of this century, and particularly that between communism and the West, have led to a multitude of interventions in the domestic affairs of states, ranging from propaganda to subversion to the use of force (covered by such doctrines as, say, Brezhnev's and Reagan's), aimed at imposing (or reestablishing) one side's view of the proper domestic order and at preventing the adversary from imposing his own.

A third trend appeared not in the realm of traditional interests but in that of ideas. On the one hand, the delegitimization of colonialism—a phenomenon accelerated by the Second World War and reenforced by the for once converging ideologies of the U.S. and the Soviet Union—led the General Assembly of the UN to remove, in effect, colonies from the domestic jurisdiction of the colonial powers (even if the UN treated the larger powers more gently than the smaller ones). The UN also declared that apartheid in South Africa and the unilateral declaration of independence by Rhodesia were threats to peace. On the other hand, the atrocities of the Second World War awakened an increasing concern for human rights, considered as a legitimate matter for international action (to be somehow conciliated with the norm of sovereignty).

These long-term trends have led not only to an *erosion* of traditional sovereignty, i.e., to a reduction in the autonomy of the state and in its actual power, but also to a striking *diffusion* of the state's influence beyond the borders of the sovereign state: through the mechanisms of the world economy and the operations of international and regional organizations, states have an increasing capacity to affect others, either deliberately (as when, say, Nigeria expels hundreds of thousands of foreign workers, or when Kuwait throws out hundreds of thousands of Palestinians, or when Germany changes its policy on asylum), or as result of its domestic policies and practices. States can easily export mischief, so to speak, by dumping refugees or economic migrants on neighbors, by training terrorists or polluting other people's rivers, etc.

Interdependence continues to affect state sovereignty in the new phase of international relations which began with the fading away of the cold war. But, in this phase, some new trends have appeared. First, instead of strong states violating the sovereignty of weaker ones in order to expand or preserve their ideology and power positions, the world is now faced with different manifestations of what might be called "people power" revolting against the existing states:[6] I refer to the sudden explosion of demands for self-determination, at the expense of the former Soviet Union and Yugoslavia principally but not exclusively (cf. Kashmir, the Kurds, the Tamils, etc.). Whereas self-determination in the era of decolonization created new states, the new wave, still aimed at creating new ones, begins by destroying existing "sovereign" units. But the problem of "weak" states is not limited to those which are racked or wrecked by demands for secession or for ethnic or religious autonomy. It extends to many of the states established in the former areas of imperial control or influence, especially in Africa—states too weak to feed their people, or too ravaged by civil wars to maintain a minimum of order: failed sovereigns.[7]

Secondly, the growth of international consciousness about the limits of sovereignty and the deficiency of a legal order dedicated primarily to its preservation has accelerated. There is increasing awareness of the dangers which a variety of state domestic policies may create for other states, in areas as diverse as the production of weapons of mass destruction, drugs, or the training of terrorists. We also witness a triple evolution of the idea of human rights. In particularly serious cases, the protection of elementary rights can now override the traditional norm of nonintervention (Iraq, Somalia). Also, the protection of minorities—neglected after the fiasco of the post-Versailles attempts—is again a major concern, given the impossibility, in most cases, of producing "pure" nation-states. Finally, there is what has been called "the emerging right to democratic governance."[8] Increasingly, individuals are seen as having not merely a right to a *state* providing a modicum of law and order, but also a right to a *nation-state* (providing that sense of community and togetherness which is national consciousness), a right to *democratic government* (national self-determination and democratic autonomy being the two faces of the right to self-governance which nineteenth-century liberals such as Mazzini and Mill had celebrated), and finally, fundamental human rights that are, so to speak, beyond any government's regulation, and need to be protected against any violations. Not only are there obvious tensions and contradictions, in practice, between these rights,[9] but the latter three challenge the present system of sovereign states and would indeed challenge any other configuration of sovereign states as well—unless the world became a paradise of satisfied, democratically governed nation-states respecting the rights of minorities and individuals.

This brief sketch points to one important conclusion for students of international relations. We have all been shaped by the dominant school of the past half century, Realism—whether we embraced it, amended it, or resisted it. Realism has looked at international politics as a distinctive "game" with rules of its own, different from those of domestic politics, and resulting from the "Hobbesian" situation of power competition in anarchy. In this view, conflict is natural, and it is cooperation that needs to be explained. State sovereignty is a central concept; the combination of sovereignty and of nonintervention (i.e., the British conception that prevailed over that of Metternich and the tsar in the European Concert set up after Napoleon's fall) provides the key legal norms; and the balance of power is the key political mechanism for the maintenance of order. We now need to reexamine the dominance of Realism (and of its contemporary variant, neo-realism, which emphasizes the way in which the structure of the international system, i.e., the distribution of power among states, shapes their possibilities and policies). More, much more is going on in international relations. We need to reconnect what happens in relations among states and what happens within states. For the fragile world order of sovereign states is threatened not only by the recurrent ambitions of would-be hegemons, but also by the effects of events that occur in states: demands for self-determination and democratic government, or the creation of domestic free markets whose agents link up across borders.

Thus state sovereignty has to be reexamined in a dual light. On the one hand, it is and remains a legal and moral norm of protection against outside interference and domination, set up in reaction against the medieval system of overlapping jurisdictions and dispersed possessions (hence the importance of continuous territory for rule in the post-Westphalian system). On the other hand, the rise of external sovereignty also accompanied another, internal development: the rise of the absolute monarchy, freed of papal and imperial claims as well as of domestic fetters, theorized by Bodin and Hobbes. The external and internal faces of sovereignty were sufficiently independent of one another to allow the Swiss Confederation, or liberal polities such as Britain and the U.S., to claim full international sovereignty. But domestic currents and international ones always had a reciprocal influence. In the system of sovereign states, when the absolute monarchy became discredited, what often replaced it was the notion of *national* sovereignty, the Rousseauistic concept that transferred internal sovereignty from the monarch to the people, first in France and later elsewhere, when it became a war machine against existing multinational states (Austria-Hungary, the Ottoman and Russian Empires) or the matrix of new sovereign national states (Italy, Germany). Conceptions of absolute sovereignty thus existed in both dimensions.

Today, many of the factors of erosion of external sovereignty have domestic origins; they represent the "spillover" into the international system of the liberal democratization of the polity. It is facilitated by that very diffusion of state influence to which we referred above; it operates through the world "market of ideas" and through the world network of institutions set up along liberal democratic lines. The idea that just as the absolute power of the sovereign at home—king or people—had to be curbed, restrained, and made accountable, the power of the sovereign state in international relations has to be limited in key areas and monitored or supervised by international agencies, represents such a "spillover."

In a world that bears little resemblance to the model of closed colliding sovereignties, the problem of intervention in domestic affairs is obviously as important, politically, legally, and morally, as the problems of inter-state conflict to which the theoretical literature, the Covenant of the League, and the Charter of the UN have addressed themselves. Indeed, it is likely to be the source of many if not most inter-state conflicts.

Insofar as many daily interventions (such as, say, that of the Bundesbank in the economies of states tied to Germany's currency) are the inevitable concomitant of economic and environmental interdependence, the way of dealing with the equally inevitable harms and inequities is through international regulation, which is not the subject of this chapter. Here, we want to consider interventions in domestic affairs which are of a coercive nature (i.e., resisted by the target) or undertaken in order to put an end to a situation of domestic chaos or turbulence in which the existing government does not have the authority to speak for the community or the power to be obeyed.

The basic moral consideration is the need to keep in mind the two conflicting sides of sovereignty from the viewpoint of the individual, which is our perspective. On the one hand, it is only too easy for liberal intellectuals in liberal polities to see the erosion of sovereignty as a form of progress—a long overdue remedy against all the crimes of neglect and of commission inflicted on human beings by their own governments in violation of their rights, and against the ability of governments protected by the shibboleth of sovereignty to plot crimes against neighbors and to pursue policies that will inflict harm and pain on people beyond their jurisdiction. It is true that, under certain conditions, outside intervention can provide such a remedy. But on the other hand, it remains true that many people, even when they are dissatisfied with and engaged in a struggle against their government, are deeply suspicious of outside interference, unwilling to substitute one form of intrusion into their lives for another, or at least hostile to foreigners who claim a right to intrude in order to protect what may well be unpopular minorities against oppressive majorities, or a right to censor a popular domestic policy in order to protect foreigners. Liberal democratization may have been creeping into international relations; but domestic nationalism as well as various forms of domestic illiberalism constitute barriers to the expansion of the role of foreign actors and of international agencies into domestic affairs.

Thus, the task of the moralist here must consist in weighing conflicting moral claims. Sometimes the claims of foreigners endangered by the domestic policies of a state must be weighed against the claims of that state's subjects; sometimes the claims of the internal victims of a government's acts must be weighed against those of the government's supporters. Sometimes the claims of a group to self-determination must be assessed against the virtues of international order, stability, and peace, which might easily be destroyed if self-determination were defined as an automatic right of any group that demands it to full sovereignty, including the right to impose its standards on minorities within the new state who could appeal for support to outside protectors. Some of the reasons for the strong emphasis of governments—and often of their people—on nonintervention, and for the "legalist paradigm," remain valid: in a world of states, sovereignty protects one against outsiders trying to topple the government or to set up a puppet regime or to impose their views of what is good and right—hence the particularly strong attachment of countries recently liberated from colonial rule to the principle of nonintervention.

Moreover, many interventions are likely to be selfish, and even if

they claim "just cause," they are likely to affect negatively the political independence of the target country. Especially when force is
used, and even if the cause is a good one—self-determination or
democratic government—outside "help" may seriously damage the
moral autonomy of the "helped." The fact that outside intervention
interferes with the activities of a state's government is not ipso facto
evil, since these activities may well be evil themselves. But the intervener may not be any better, and even when he is, both his motives and his effects may be wrong. On the other hand, there are
many cases in which the effects of nonintervention might be worse
than those of intervention, either on political or on moral grounds:
let us think of the cases of Bangla-Desh, Idi Amin, and Pol Pot—
three cases in which the outside intervener argued in terms of self-
defense in order to appear in conformity with a UN Charter rooted
in sovereignty. A world in which the norm of nonintervention
would be rigidly enforced would be one of fragmented chaos, and
the bad examples of domestic mischief, left intact, could all too easily spread. Neither justice nor peace would be served, as the members of the Security Council Summit in 1992 recognized when they
acknowledged that changes in a state's structure, policies of nuclear
proliferation, and nonmilitary sources of insecurity can constitute
threats to peace.

The task for thinkers and statesmen is therefore complex. They
must maintain and even raise barriers to illegitimate intervention,
define the areas, conditions, and procedures for legitimate ones, pay
particular attention in both sets of cases to the special problems
raised by coercion, particularly forcible coercion, and proceed as
much as possible on a broad basis of consent; i.e., they must keep
in mind the reasons for and rules of the state system, while attempting to change it. What does this mean in practice? I would suggest
a double task. On the one hand, it is necessary to restrict the scope
of unilateral and self-interested state intervention, especially forcible
ones. This is for the general reasons indicated in an essay by Michael
Smith,[10] among which the protection of the target's autonomy is
particularly important. As for interventions by force, even when a
state invokes a righteous cause—democracy, human rights, national
self-determination—not only are several of these notions open to

conflicting interpretations, but a cause is not always a motive or intention, and the likelihood of self-seeking purposes is great. The justice of a use of force is not determined by the cause alone; one has to look at the historical origins of the resort to force, at the actual political ends, at the appropriateness of the means to the ends, at proportionality, at the long-term effects on the target, etc. The old *presumption* against unilateral intervention ought to stand.

On the other hand, given the number and importance of cases in which nonintervention would neither serve justice nor preserve world order, it is necessary to concentrate on collective interventions: when are they legitimate, and how can they be organized in such a way as to provide as much impartiality as possible? In interstate affairs, the Charter expresses a broad consensus on the idea that threats to peace, breaches of peace, and acts of aggression constitute "community causes" that legitimize the collective intervention of the Security Council. The equivalent to such causes, in domestic affairs, would be, first, domestic policies and practices capable of leading to serious threats to peace or aggressions, and, secondly, grave violations of human rights; and the underlying idea is that the norm of the formal equality of states, which is the twin of the norm of nonintervention, can legitimately be dented when a state seriously violates such principles as the right to self-determination, to democratic government, to life, etc., or behaves at home in a way that creates international disorder.

How are such very general ideas to be made capable of providing moral and political guidance? Let us try to develop maxims that should aim at our chosen end, the protection and development of the individual and of his rights in a fragmented world, and provide an objective principle valid for all rational beings. Such maxims should be acceptable by all states that are based on the citizens' consent and respect their human rights. We must also see whether the social order that would result from these maxims is one which the actors could will. Insofar as *unilateral* interventions are concerned, a maxim that would allow them (including forcible ones) for such "good" causes as self-determination, democratic government, and the protection of elementary human rights would not be acceptable, even if such actions were to be undertaken only by democratic

states, because of one insoluble problem: the absence of an impartial
agency that determines that the cause is good and assures that the
intervener has no other motive than the enforcement of what is
right. On the other hand, a maxim banning all forcible, unilateral
interventions, while it might often improve global social order,
would not always do so, and could be highly detrimental to a value
that is at least as respectable as peace and order: justice, by allowing
grave injustices to persist. Thus, we have to move to the second stage
of our procedure, and reintroduce the complexities of reality.

A more practical ethics suggests the following prescriptions:

(a) In cases where what we have called "community causes" for
interventions in domestic affairs are at stake, unilateral coercive intervention should be deemed legitimate only if licensed by the UN,
or by a regional organization operating with UN consent, after non-
coercive remedies have been exhausted, when "the violation will
cause irreparable injury" and when "the intervention is calculated
to cause less damage to the target society than would inaction";[11]
or, if the UN has been incapable of dealing with such an issue, and
whatever regional organization empowered to deal with it has also
demonstrated its paralysis or impotence—as in the cases of Tanza-
nia's removal of Idi Amin from Uganda, and of Vietnam's intervention against Pol Pot.

(b) The decision by a government to subordinate its economic
assistance to the willingness of the beneficiary to protect human
rights or to move toward granting its people the right to self-determination or to democratic government would also be deemed legitimate; so would a decision to suspend or end any aid to a government that violates one of the "community causes."

(c) Assistance to a democratically elected government that fights
a rebellion, especially one supported from the outside, would also
be legitimate. This would also be true of a counter-intervention
aimed at preventing a foreign-backed force from imposing its will
on a resisting or hostile population—especially when this force
would be most unlikely to prevail without external assistance—as
long as the counter-intervention observes the restraints required by
traditional *jus in bello* and aims not at a military victory but at a
political solution.

If these criteria had been adopted, they would have eliminated as illegitimate the American interventions in Guatemala, Grenada, Panama, even in El Salvador, and certainly in Nicaragua. But since the causes of legitimate unilateral intervention are always open to distortion, the intervening state ought to submit its actions to the UN and to the relevant regional organization, for explanation and if possible for endorsement.

Insofar as *collective* intervention is concerned, far less thought has been given to it during the years when the cold war paralyzed the UN over broad ranges of issues. What would be needed now is, in the first place, providing a normative basis for legitimate collective action, a *jus ad interventionem*. Our "universal maxim" has already been stated: it allows for collective intervention when a state's condition or behavior results in grave threats to other states' and peoples' peace and security, and in grave and massive violations of human rights. There is another way of phrasing it. Sovereignty can be seen, both in Hobbes' and in Locke's versions of the social contract, as a kind of contract by which the state promises to guarantee the members of society against outside intrusions; both in exchange for this protection, and as a way of assuring it, the state allows foreign agents to operate within its borders only at its own request or with its consent. But sovereignty can be overridden whenever the behavior of the state even within its own territory threatens the existence of elementary human rights abroad, and whenever the protection of the rights of its own members can be assured only from the outside.

Two *Grundnormen* on which this maxim rests exist already. One is the protection of human rights, enshrined in a variety of documents, and especially the protection of the right to life and to physical integrity, recognized by both of the UN Human Rights Covenants. The other one is the right of states and people to peace and security—without which those human rights will not be tenable. But a more precise "bed" of moral and legal norms derived from our maxim remains to be built. Fragile precedents have been established in recent years. Certain civil wars (Cambodia, Angola) have been treated as international conflicts, largely because of the involvement of outside powers, or also because wars for self-determination, while they break up a sovereign state, lead to the establishment of new states (Yugoslavia, where the UN, the European Union, and the Organization for Security and Cooperation in Europe have all insisted on the inviolability of existing borders, internal as well as external). Humanitarian interventions to protect mistreated or starving populations have been organized under the rubric of threats to peace (the Kurds in Iraq, Somalia). Sanctions against Libya because of its failure to extradite two suspected terrorists have been justified under the same rubric. In Iraq, for the first time, a state has been ordered to destroy its weapons of mass destruction. A complete collapse of law and order in one country—Somalia—has been deemed a threat to international peace and security by the Security Council.

Norms for community intervention need to be further developed in the following areas:

(a) The nonproliferation treaty, which is hard to revise, could be completed by a protocol strengthening the safeguards, and granting to the IAEA far more extensive and intrusive rights of inspection, allowing it to check possible diversions of finite materials for military uses.

(b) On the model of a strengthened NPT, a treaty prohibiting the sale and acquisition of certain weapons of mass destruction (some categories of conventional missiles, chemical and biological weapons) and committing its signatories not to produce such weapons, would provide the basis for comparable inspections and sanctions in cases of violations.

(c) As I have already suggested,[12] another kind of treaty would be useful: one that would define the circumstances in which collective humanitarian intervention could be authorized by a qualified majority of signatories; such operations would be reported to a treaty Secretariat and to the Security Council. The latter could request their end. The cases would include natural or man-made disasters, when the state in which they occur is indifferent or obstructive; instances in which weapons of mass destruction have been used by a state against its internal enemies; the violent persecution of whole groups within a state.

(d) In order to prevent such persecutions and to remove pretexts for unilateral outside intervention, a revival of treaties protecting ethnic, religious, and cultural minorities would be desirable. Providing minorities with extensive autonomy would both satisfy legitimate aspirations and prevent an epidemic of demands for and wars of independence. These treaties should entail a procedure for the review of grievances either by judicial bodies or by a committee of good offices set up under the treaty (and not including representatives of states whose affinity for the protected minority might lead to their manipulation of that minority from the outside). Sanctions could be imposed by the UN on states that refuse either to sign such a treaty or to provide adequate and protected rights to its minorities through domestic legislation.

(e) Another treaty or protocol under UN auspices could commit states where a serious breakdown of government occurs to request UN intervention for what the Secretary General has called peace-building. This intervention could take several forms, depending on the degree of chaos, and range from extensive assistance to temporary rule (see note 7).

(f) Still in the realm of human rights, but more broadly, the members of the UN ought to sign a protocol allowing the Secretary General to report on and require collective action about violations of human rights with potentially disastrous effects because the position and resources of the state that commits them, and / or the preparations for aggressive war made by its leader, create high risks for other states, or when such violations, if left unsanctioned, could become incentives to unilateral external intervention.

(g) It has been suggested[13] that the new governments of states which result from the exercise of the right to self-determination should authorize the international community that recognizes them to intervene during a certain period in order to assure the country's compliance with recognition criteria that include commitments to democracy and the respect of individual and minority rights.

Norms are indispensable but insufficient. Enforcement is essential. Here we encounter both a principle and a paradox. The principle is the superiority of prevention over repression, because all means of coercion, whether economic or military, risk inflicting indiscriminate harm on innocents and causing far more discomfort to the led than to the leaders. The paradox is that, so far, prevention has been easier, juridically, for the international community in matters of inter-state conflicts (under Chapter VI and VII of the Charter) than in cases of domestic turmoil, precisely because of the strength of the norm protecting a state's domestic jurisdiction. As recent examples have shown, once the international community mobilizes itself to cope with atrocities against human rights and with threats to peace originating in domestic practices, it may be too late to help the victims.

Prevention in domestic affairs could take a variety of forms. The most obvious is diplomacy: international good offices, when domestic tensions could lead to civil wars, indeed, attempts at conflict resolution when such tensions could result both in civil wars and in external entanglements (cf. Nagorno-Karabakh). Such diplomatic efforts may be undertaken by private actors and organizations, who may be more acceptable and appear less intrusive to troubled governments than public actors, and could work in more discreet and informal conditions. Another form would be internal economic and financial assistance to help countries whose economic conditions could provoke massive flows of economic refugees, or to help certain countries move away from their reliance on the production and export of drugs. The various treaties mentioned above would institute preventive mechanisms of inspection or for the adjudication of grievances. The Secretary General of the UN has also argued for "preventive deployment" of a UN force at the request of the government or all parties concerned, or with their consent, in "conditions of national crisis."[14] One could imagine that in such a case the force, once deployed, could not be removed without the consent of the Security Council (cf. the precedent of UNPROFOR in Yugoslavia).

If prevention fails, violations of treaties are detected, or a government opposes a legitimate humanitarian intervention, there is a need to think of sanctions that are less likely than others to fall on the innocent. The assistance often provided by international and regional bodies to a government could be suspended, and if civil wars are treated more like inter-state conflicts, sanctions against the (more) guilty party could increase the costs of aggressive war.

Often, one will have to go beyond sanctions, and provide one or all three of the kinds of international forces that may be indispensable: unarmed or lightly armed peace-*keepers* deployed after an agreement by all the parties has been reached; peace-*enforcers*, whenever there is no genuine consent of all the parties and the operation, or the execution of the agreement reached under international jurisdiction requires the use of force to protect the international contingents from attack and to allow them to carry out their mission;[15] genuine *war fighting* forces under Article 43, "useful . . . in meeting any military force" other than that of a major modern army. Such forces ought to be capable of resorting to air strikes against military targets in a variety of "domestic" cases (genocide, dangerous nuclear buildups, state terrorism, etc.).[16]

The consequences in the "real world" of the maxims proposed, of the norms suggested, and of the means of enforcement envisaged, would be . . . a world very different from the present one. The new order would severely restrict the capacity of states to do mischief—to their own people or to outsiders—behind the convenient barrier of sovereignty. It would considerably increase the authority and jurisdiction of international and regional organizations, and thus address the question of the gap between an eroding sovereignty (or rather its transformation, which both weakens the state's autonomy and opens new sources and channels of influence for it) and collective institutions in areas such as the economy, the environment, security, and human rights. However, the new order would still be fragile. First, that gap would not be closed: legitimate collective actions would still depend for their effectiveness on the cooperation of states. Secondly, insofar as collective institutions would have a broader sphere of legitimate action, the questions of their processes of decision and of their actual capabilities would become central. Thirdly, even if these questions are answered in a way that consolidates the impartiality of such bodies and increases their effectiveness, one could expect, in many instances, a dangerous backlash against the intrusion of international bureaucrats and soldiers and the *diktats* of foreign coalitions, not only on the part of the targeted "bad" governments, but on that of aroused domestic groups that endorse these governments' policies. To put it a bit simplistically, in a world in which cosmopolitanism remains largely the faith of (some) intellectuals and of international civil servants, and in which nationalism remains a force governments can often whip up against external intruders and unpopular minorities, the ambitious new order presented here may have a great deal of trouble getting established and preserved.

We do not doubt its desirability, and its moral superiority over an order that tolerates great evils by preserving the increasingly artificial barrier between what is "external" and what is "domestic." But we must be lucid about the obstacles our conception faces. They can be divided into four categories: the persistent gap between ethics and law, the difficulty of "universalizing" the key criteria for action, ethical difficulties of execution, and practical obstacles to collective intervention.

Traditional international law has been hostile not only to unilateral intervention in domestic affairs, but also to collective coercive action *except* in cases of threats to peace, breaches of peace, and aggression. Tom Farer is right in pointing out that for the "founding fathers," humanitarian intervention was illegal.[17] The greatest recent progress has been the willingness of the Security Council to broaden the tent of "threats to peace." But is the protection of the Kurds the application of a new principle of humanitarian intervention on behalf of oppressed minorities, or a simple extension of the classical collective security operation against Iraq, that would never have occurred if Iraq had not invaded Kuwait? (It certainly was not a recognition of the right to self-determination, since the UN proclaimed its respect for Iraq's territorial integrity.) Many of the recent collective interventions in weak states have occurred, formally at least, at the request of the state concerned or of all the parties involved (Angola, Yugoslavia, El Salvador, Mozambique, even Somalia in early 1992, Cambodia). Only the OAS, so far, has gone beyond violations of minority rights, or emergency relief intervention, or the monitoring of elections (as by the UN in Namibia, Angola, Western Sahara, Cambodia), all the way to attempts at restoring democracy (Haiti). The Secretary General has preferred linking the UN monitoring of elections in Nicaragua to Central American peace efforts rather than to human rights, and whether Somalia and

Cambodia will be the first in a series of temporary takeovers of "failed states," or exceptions, will depend on the fate of the two operations. So far—wisely perhaps, as Adam Roberts suggests[18]— the UN has resisted endorsing a general doctrine; it has proceeded case by case. This means not only that the normative scene remains far poorer than the one we advocated above, but also that the extent to which it has moved beyond the traditional one remains in doubt. Even the extension of "threats to peace" is ambiguous: does it mean that violations of human rights are to trigger coercive measures only when—as in the Middle East or the Balkans—such outrages are indeed likely to provoke inter-state conflicts, or does it mean that (like apartheid) grave violations are seen as ipso facto threats to peace? If the former interpretation is the right one, many atrocities—as in East Timor or Tibet—might go unsanctioned. But the society of states may well not be ready for, and not deem desirable, the latter version.[19]

The second group of difficulties concerns the concepts on which legitimate international intervention in domestic issues may be based. Providing a universally acceptable definition is no easier here than in the familiar case of "aggression." Four examples can be given. The first is the notion of *self-determination*. Is it a fundamental human right? There are divergent notions of nationhood; the democratic one ties together the two forms of self-government, i.e., national autonomy and democratic autonomy, but there are authoritarian and organic conceptions as well which deny the individuals any say in the "choice" of their nation. Moreover, from the viewpoint of international order, self-determination has a profoundly destructive and explosive force, if the "self" that wants autonomy is any group of people that considers itself maltreated (even a recourse to history in order to see whether the group has been coerced into incorporation in a state does not begin to solve the problem, given the history of most states!).[20] And from the viewpoint of international justice, in areas where ethnic and religious groups are mixed together, we find conflicting claims: in the former Yugoslavia, the claim of the Bosnian plurality to a separate state has—quite apart from the Serbs' resort to violence—been better received than the claim of the Serbs in Bosnia (or in Croatia) to their own right of

self-determination and their refusal to be a minority in the new
states resulting from Yugoslavia's disintegration. To be sure, minority treaties and plebiscites could help make the claims less irrecon-
cilable, but not everyone's demand for full autonomy can be recognized.

Things are not any clearer with the concept of *democracy* as a just
cause for intervention. What is meant by it? Is it simply the holding
and supervision of elections? They are a first step, but especially after
protracted civil wars and in areas without democratic experience,
the aftermath could be renewed violence—*vide* Angola and Cambodia. Should there be a norm of legitimate collective intervention
for the restoration of democracy where it has been overthrown by
force? Should this be limited to cases where the overthrown government had been established with the help of an international or
regional organization (as in Haiti), or extended beyond such cases?
Should there be an even more ambitious norm of "democratic entitlement," based on the idea of the connection between democracy
and peace, and on the idea that democracy is the regime that best
protects human rights? Even those of us who believe in those arguments realize that democracy is both a complex set of norms, procedures, and institutions, and far more than just a set of norms,
procedures, and institutions; therefore either the protection or the
creation of democracy is not an easily definable and enforceable notion.

This is why the maxim recommended above mentioned explicitly
neither democracy nor self-determination, but serious violations of
human rights, among which the rights to a national community and
to a democratic government can be found. However, the concept of
human rights is not any easier to define, beyond a probable consensus
on the right to physical integrity and life, and a practical recognition
of the fact that the latter cannot become a cause for collective concern and intervention unless it is being violated on a grand scale.
But how grand is grand? And what about other rights?

The fourth example is that of *domestic policies* capable of threatening peace and security outside. One can argue that this is an ex-
ceedingly subjective notion: some governments are likely to find
themselves more threatened than others, depending on their states'

power, on their political makeup, on the volatility of their public, and on the state of their relations with, or of their ambitions aimed at, the "culprit." Can anyone, then, ring the alarm bell? Aren't almost any policies that have effects beyond borders—policies on the environment, on national defense, in imports and exports, on population movements and citizenship, etc. (i.e., most policies) capable of being perceived as threats by others? Or should one limit the possibility of ringing the alarm bell to cases where the state's domestic practices or policies violate international agreements signed by it? This would suffer from the opposite flaw, by leaving enormous loopholes for internal mischief with external effects. These are the kinds of questions which are almost insoluble in the abstract, and explain why international law and the UN proceed case by case.

The third category of obstacles is formed by the ethical dilemmas, not of conceptualization and definition, but of execution. Three examples can be taken up here. The first is the case against the sudden enthusiasm for humanitarian intervention. Adam Roberts, in a recent lecture (see note 18), uses much incisive wit to make two strong charges. One is that of the slippery slope: the risk of the UN finding itself trapped, by the circumstances of civil war and chaos, into military involvement at the end of the road, when it becomes the only way to fulfill the original objectives of what had begun as mere relief for the victims (he mentions, of course, Yugoslavia and Somalia). The second argument is that humanitarian action can be an alibi, an escape from politics. Many humanitarian disasters—particularly those that produce masses of refugees—result not from "acts of God" but from political turmoil or violence; as long as the roots of such humanitarian disasters have not been torn out, the agony may not only persist, but be prolonged by the failure to go to those roots. Bosnia, perhaps Somalia (if the factions are not disarmed), the Kurds (to whom UN "relief" provides not only food but a protection for de facto autonomy that remains fragile as long as Saddam Hussein's regime surrounds them) are examples.[21] This charge reminds one—for better or worse—of Sartre's indictment of Camus's "Red Cross ethics," as developed in *The Plague* and applied, unhappily, by Camus in the Algerian War.

Ernst Haas has sketched a comparable case against collective in-

tervention for democracy.[22] Even if one could agree on what such
intervention should aim at establishing or restoring, one would have
to confront John Stuart Mill's (and Walzer's) argument that democracy—unlike national self-determination—cannot be provided by
outsiders: the latter requires merely the end of alien rule, which may
well in turn require external help for liberation, but democratic government requires practices and mores that can only be indigenous.
Foreigners can draft laws and constitutions, but only the "natives"
can put substance into such "envelopes" (a term used by de Gaulle
about constitutions); and even when well-intentioned, outsiders
don't ever know enough to succeed, unless the seeds of democracy
exist already, and the various psychological, social, and economic
preconditions are met.

The next case is that of the means of coercion. As we have already
stated, economic sanctions can create humanitarian disasters, because of the great difficulty of selective targeting. Sanctions can also
exacerbate existing imbalances if they are applied equally to parties,
one of which is much stronger than the other;[23] this has been the
problem with the arms embargo on the former Yugoslavia, which
has helped mighty Serbia at the expense of Bosnia. As for armed
collective interventions, they risk running into all the moral objections to modern war: even when the requirements of proportionality and chance of success are met, noncombatant immunity is likely
to be a casualty, as was demonstrated again in Iraq despite all efforts
not to target civilians directly. Even if force is merely deployed, and
not used, it often has a profoundly corrupting effect in countries
where poverty and chaos reign and where the military occupiers and
protectors have large amounts of money to throw around.

Finally, there are obstacles constituted by the politics of intervention—all of which, obviously, have ethical aspects and effects. A
first obstacle is the problem of political support. On the one hand
there is continuing resistance to intervention—unilateral or collective—by many states marked by their colonial experience; India and
Latin America come to mind. This resistance is probably stronger
against attempts to "police" domestic behavior than in cases of civil
war and chaos (Serbia's brutalization of Bosnia has produced shock
waves not only among Muslim states but among small states in gen-

eral). But the fact that many states have skeletons in their closets with respect to human rights (the UN resolution that condemned Iraqi repression of the Kurds could not invoke Chapter VII because of China's objections), and that in particular many new states have—like India—formidable problems with ethnic or religious minorities, explains this resistance to any brushing aside of the traditional norm of nonintervention. The more coercive the attempted collective intervention will be, the more problematic the likelihood of compliance: economic sanctions, in the Serbian case, have been sieves, and the closer one gets to the model of collective security, the more apparent become the traditional flaws of a strategy that demands of states that they put the enforcement of abstract general norms ahead of power interests or of transnational solidarities, as Russia's hesitation to get tough on Serbia has shown. On the other hand, international and regional organizations find it difficult to act unless a strong impulse is given by a major power. The U.S. initiatives to protect the Kurds in Iraq and to promote the return of President Aristide in Haiti, and the American intervention in Somalia, are cases in point: they have activated the international community. It is Nigeria which has dominated the West African intervention in Liberia. The counterexample is Yugoslavia, where the OSCE essentially was forced by its rule of unanimity to leave the problem to the EC, which dumped it on the UN—where the call for multilateral action became a cloak for collective impotence.

Thus too expansive a maxim allowing for collective intervention is likely to result in embarrassing failures to act and fiascoes in action. It is also likely to run into a second obstacle: the problem of consistency or double standards. At this point, the UN lacks the possibility even to conceive of a coercive intervention in the domestic affairs of a major power, either in the "North" or in a given region (Russian moves to protect non-Georgians in Georgia and to crush Chechnia's secession have not been treated like Serb actions in Croatia or Bosnia, and Chinese oppression of Tibet has not led to any sanctions). The taboo on borders which the UN and above all the OAU have maintained in Africa, which led to the refusal to grant the right of self-determination to Biafra and to a lack of external support for Eritrea's efforts, has not been applied in Yugoslavia (to

compare only cases of secession resisted by the former "master").
Violations of human and minority rights have been treated with
selective inattention: "ethnic cleansing" was, in a way, tolerated in
Kuwait (at the Palestinians' expense) but not in Bosnia, the Shiites
in Southern Iraq were not treated like Kurds in the South, nor were
the Kurds in Turkey. UNPROFOR has remained neutral between
Croatia and Serbia (whose cease-fire the UN force was supposed to
preserve) despite Croatian and Serbian violations; but the UN operation in Cambodia (UNTAC) risks becoming embroiled in a war
against the Khmer Rouge, just as the West African forces in Liberia
became a party in the civil war that is wrecking that country. How
much attention is paid to what case, in a world in which internal
chaos and atrocities are so frequent and weak states so numerous,
depends largely on the media: where they place their spotlight, action is far more likely to follow than where they do not—and this
is of course a powerful incentive for mischief-making governments
to keep them out or in the dark.

A last obstacle is the problem of collective capabilities. The UN
lacks the necessary equipment for adequate prevention (it would require, as we have stated, a huge increase of its domestic fact-finding
capabilities, through monitoring and inspecting), and it has neither
the peace-enforcers that Secretary General Boutros-Ghali has been
calling for (volunteers from member states, on call, "with their
terms of reference specified in advance"), nor have the provisions of
Article 43 been put into effect. When there is no local agreement
calling for a UN presence (as in Somalia) or when the agreement
breaks down (as in Cambodia and constantly in Bosnia), UN forces
are thus at the mercy of local factions. Often, the amount of force
that would be needed to safeguard those whom the operation aims
at protecting—the Kurds in Iraq, or the Bosnians—would have to
be huge in order to overcome formidable logistical difficulties.[24]

The point of this long litany of conceptual, moral, and political
difficulties is not to show that we are outside the domain of moral
obligation, because reality blocks any attempt at applying the maxims we have recommended and because where there is no "can"
there is no valid "ought." Some progress has already been made,

such as the recent extensions of "threats to peace" to a variety of domestic matters, and inconsistent collective interventions are better than none at all. But what is obvious is the need to clarify the implications of the different and woolly concepts that will define the "good" causes, and to establish a hierarchy of concerns so as to make it possible to deal with the contradictions between the four notions of sovereignty, self-determination, democratic government, and individual rights. What is needed just as urgently is an increase in the financial and operational capabilities of international and regional organizations; for the only alternatives to it are likely to be either indifference to domestic calamities that may often be dismissed as not grave or close enough to threaten the physical security of the greater powers—and as a result of such indifference, risk spreading by imitation and contagion—or else a return to unilateral intervention that could be even more dangerous for stability and for justice. As for the problem of support and the real danger of domestic backlash in the countries that are the targets of intervention, one way of addressing them is to make sure that the collective interventions are fair, remain within the limits of a clear mandate, and do not appear as the tools of certain powers.

NOTES

1. Lori Fisler Damrosch, "Changing Conceptions of Intervention in International Law," paper for a conference of the American Academy of Arts and Sciences, January 1993.
2. Ibid., 6.
3. See Michael Walzer, *Just and Unjust Wars* (New York: Basic Books, 1977), 58.
4. Morton Halperin and David Scheffer with Patricia Small, *Self-Determination in the New World Order* (Washington: Carnegie Endowment, 1992), 20.
5. See Robert Keohane's essay, "Sovereignty, Interdependence, and International Institutions," in *Ideas and Ideals,* ed. Linda Miller and Michael Joseph Smith (Boulder, Colo.: Westview Press, 1993), 91–107.
6. Stanley Hoffmann, "A New World and Its Troubles," in *Seachanges,*

ed. Nicholas Rizopoulos (New York: Council on Foreign Relations, 1990), 274–92.

7. Gerald Helman and Steven Ratner, "Saving Failed States," *Foreign Policy* (Winter 1992–93): 3–20.

8. Thomas M. Franck, "The Emerging Right to Democratic Governance," *American Journal of International Law* 86, no. 1 (January 1992): 46–91.

9. Stanley Hoffmann, "The Delusions of World Order," *New York Review of Books* 39, no. 7, 9 April 1992, 37–42.

10. Michael Smith, "Ethics and Intervention," *Ethics and International Affairs* 3 (1989): 1–26.

11. Tom Farer, "A Paradigm of Legitimate Intervention," in *Enforcing Restraint*, ed. Lori Fisler Damrosch (New York: Council on Foreign Relations Press, 1993), 327.

12. Hoffmann, "The Delusions of World Order." See also David J. Scheffer, "Toward a Modern Doctrine of Humanitarian Intervention," *University of Toledo Law Review* 23, no. 2 (Winter 1992): 253–93.

13. Halperin and Scheffer, *Self-Determination*, 91.

14. "An Agenda for Peace," report of the Secretary General, Boutros-Ghali, pursuant to the statement adopted by the Summit Meeting of the Security Council on 31 January 1992, 16–17.

15. Farer, "A Paradigm of Legitimate Intervention," 20; Elgin Clemons, "Blue Helmet Peace-keeping in Situations of Active Conflict," background paper for the New York University Conference on the future of UN collective security, January 1993, 46–48.

16. Boutros-Ghali, "An Agenda for Peace," 25.

17. Tom Farer, "An Inquiry into the Legitimacy of Humanitarian Intervention," in *Law and Force in the New International Order*, ed. Lori Fisler Damrosch and David J. Scheffer (Boulder, Colo.: Westview Press, 1991), 185–201.

18. Adam Roberts, "Humanitarian War: Military Intervention and Human Rights," lecture at Keele University, 26 February 1993.

19. Lori Fisler Damrosch, "Commentary on Collective Military Intervention to Enforce Human Rights," in Damrosch and Scheffer, *Law and Force*, 216–23.

20. Halperin and Scheffer, *Self-Determination*, 77.

21. Jane Stromseth, "Iraq," in Damrosch, *Enforcing Restraint*, 93.

22. Ernst Haas, "Beware the Slippery Slope: Notes toward a Definition of Justifiable Intervention," in *Emerging Norms of Justified Intervention*, ed. Laura W. Reed and Carl Kaysen (Cambridge, Mass.: American Academy of Arts and Sciences, 1993), 63–87.

23. Lori Fisler Damrosch, "The Civilian Impact of Economic Sanctions," in Damrosch, *Enforcing Restraint,* 274–315.

24. Richard Falk, "Human Rights, Humanitarian Assistance and the Sovereignty of States," paper for a conference cosponsored by the Center for International Health and Cooperation and the Council on Foreign Relations, September 1992.

3

HUMANITARIAN INTERVENTION IN THE FORMER YUGOSLAVIA

Stanley Hoffmann

THE CASE OF Yugoslavia is an important one for students of intervention in general and humanitarian intervention in particular. It is one of those sad cases in international affairs where everything that can go wrong goes wrong. Just as doctors are said from time to time to be particularly enamored of beautiful diseases, so for political scientists this is, alas, an extremely informative case. It is a case of collective intervention, the very issue for which I was trying to find criteria in my first lecture—collective intervention made possible by the disintegration of Yugoslavia. I will not go into a recital of the facts, which have been well covered elsewhere,[1] but I will allude to some.

Throughout 1990 it became clear that the Yugoslav Federation was beginning to disintegrate; in particular, Slovenia and Croatia were taking steps toward secession and were warning that they would secede. Attempts at shoring up this crumbling federation did not get anywhere; it is not as if there had been no advance notice. Then, in the summer of 1991, the secession of Croatia and Slovenia

This essay is based on a lecture delivered in January 1995; it covers events prior to the NATO bombings that began late in August 1995 and led to the Dayton agreements that brought peace back—for how long?—to the former Yugoslavia. Ultimately, the use of force alone (by Croatia, encouraged by the United States, and by NATO) was able to compel the Bosnian Serbs to cease their aggression. Post-Dayton events show that the U.S. remains more worried by the risk of "mission creep" than by the possibility of either renewed violence or formal partition of Bosnia, and that neither Washington nor its allies have taken seriously the demands of international criminal justice.

took place, the Yugoslavian army—mainly Serbian—went into action, and fairly rapidly a cease-fire was signed with Slovenia; war moved then, intensely, into Croatia. First, I am going to talk about the nature of the case itself, and then, about the international confusion which has been the main characteristic of this story.

There are many issues, but in particular three, which have to do with trying to fit the Yugoslavian disaster into some sort of category.

The first key issue, and the most difficult in some ways, is the issue of who is entitled to self-determination. Initially, practically all the major powers—the United States, the Soviet Union, the United Kingdom, and France—tried to keep the Yugoslavian Federation alive. The U.S. made various statements to that effect, through Secretary of State James Baker in particular. Even when the European Community, represented by Jacques Delors, the head of the Commission of the European Union, offered some economic aid, it was on condition that the Yugoslavian Federation be maintained. Why was there such an attachment to what was after all not a particularly well-functioning federation? There were two reasons. One was the fear, which was very strong in 1991, of a domino effect on the Soviet Union. All this was taking place in the spring and summer of 1991, before the coup that almost overthrew Gorbachev, when Gorbachev was trying to negotiate a new Union treaty for the USSR that would keep all the various components together; there certainly was a very strong fear, especially in much of Western Europe and in Washington, that to accept the secession of Slovenia and Croatia would have a snowballing effect on countries like Ukraine. This was the time when President Bush sternly warned the Ukrainians not to declare independence. The major concern of everybody was the fate of the Soviet Union, rather than that of Yugoslavia.

The second reason was the awareness of all the statesmen that there was an insoluble problem of minorities. However you cut the cake, there was no way of having an independent state carved out of Yugoslavia that would not have a formidable problem of minorities within its borders. Under those circumstances was it not better to keep a perhaps elusive federation or at least a federation in which the minorities in one country could feel that they had some advocates within the central organs of the federation? This and a number of other factors explain why there was very little preventive action. I have talked about the superiority of prevention; here, there was practically no prevention. The UN could not do very much since nobody brought the problem to it before the fall of 1991, when the war was already raging.

The Organization for Security and Cooperation in Europe cannot function except by unanimity, and the Yugoslavian government was very unwilling to let the OSCE discuss Yugoslavia's future. The Europeans had another reason for not being too vigilant: the very difficult negotiations which occupied them throughout 1991 and led in December to the Maastricht Treaty on European Union. At the end of 1990 the United States was preoccupied by the coming Gulf war, which went, in effect, to the end of April, and after that a certain sense of relief and exhaustion settled on Washington.

This attitude of indifference, this crossing of one's fingers in the hope that somehow the federation would survive, of course changed as soon as Slovenia and Croatia finally declared their independence in June. At that moment in the summer of 1991, German pressure for recognition of Slovenia and Croatia began in earnest. The secession had already taken place and Germany tried very hard to convince its partners in the European Community that it ought to recognize these new states. There were many reasons why the newly reunited Germany felt particularly strongly on the subject of self-determination, about which many of the other members of the Community had serious reservations. Yet they ended up, more or less reluctantly, siding with Germany. What became the priority within the Community was not so much the wisdom of recognition, about which there was much argument, but the maintenance of the unity of the Community. When one talks with officials of the EC, one discovers that to them the common decision reached in December, despite French and British reluctance, to recognize collectively in the near future the independence of Croatia and Slovenia was seen as a victory for the EC because it prevented a breach between Germany on the one hand and practically everybody else on the other. So even though many of the others had misgivings, and even though Germany ultimately jumped the gun on recognition anyhow, a facade of unity was maintained. The British and the

French swallowed their misgivings because recognition came surrounded by a variety of legal formulas, thanks to the establishment of an arbitration commission which set some conditions for recognition. These were met in the case of Slovenia, but recognition of Croatia came even though the Croatian Government had not met all of the conditions (concerning minority rights). Of course, the recognition of Slovenia and Croatia first by the Europeans, then by the United States, only displaced the problem. The question then became very quickly, why should the Croats and the Slovenes have a right to a state of their own and not the Serbs who were in Croatia and in Bosnia-Herzegovina? The question was submitted by the Serbs to the Badinter Arbitration Commission. The latter, having declared internal borders as inviolable as international ones, declared that the right of self-determination could be claimed only by "territorially defined administrative units," such as Croatia or Bosnia, but not by minorities within such units. Precisely because there was something slightly quaint about this verdict, the solution would be to give to the Serbs, condemned to be a minority in a new state, all the guarantees for minorities which the Commission then proceeded to define. Thus, the solution would have been not full self-determination (i.e. independence) for every group that claimed it. Rather, those groups—mainly the Serbs—who found themselves suddenly a minority in Croatia and Bosnia after having been a major force within the old Yugoslavia were told to accept, in lieu of full self-determination, a fairly generous protection of minorities. This is precisely what the Serbs rejected and went to war over.

Bosnia is the most tragic case, because when Croatia and Slovenia first moved toward independence, Bosnia did not. Bosnia was a sort of replica of the Federation of Yugoslavia in the sense that it was a mix of Croats, Serbs, and Bosnian Muslims. But once Slovenia and Croatia declared their independence next to a new Yugoslavia composed of Serbia and Montenegro, what could Bosnia-Herzegovina do? It could either become a province of this new Serb-dominated Yugoslavia, which, of course, the Muslims and the Croats in Bosnia did not want; and they represented more that two-thirds of the population. Or else it could follow suit and seek an independence that it had never thought about much before, which is what hap-

pened. As indeed Bosnia's President, Alija Izetbegoviv, warned the
Europeans, (a) he had no choice but to ask for independence, (b)
that might lead to troubles given the precedent of what had happened to Croatia, and (c) therefore the Europeans or the international community ought to send some forces to his country. This
was not done. What was done was once again to set a number of
conditions which Bosnia had to meet before its independence would
be recognized. The main condition was a referendum; that referendum took place, it was boycotted by the Serbs; so one ended up with
a large majority for independence but with about 35–40 percent of
the population not taking part in the referendum. But since the referendum had taken place, a vast majority of those voting had voted
for independence, and the government of Bosnia met the conditions
set for the treatment of minorities by the Arbitration Commission, Bosnia-Herzegovina was recognized immediately both by the
United States and the European Union. Of course, as in the case
of Croatia, war broke out.

The second question has to do with the nature of that war. Is it
a civil war or is it an international conflict? If one follows the statements of American leaders, the president included, on this subject
(a slightly dizzying exercise), it seems to be a civil war on odd days
and an international war on even days. One cannot entirely blame
them, because there are clearly elements of both. One may want to
ask, why is it an important question? If it is a civil war, traditionally
the approach of the so-called international community, the UN in
particular, is not that it is condemned to nonintervention. We should
remember the Congo crisis of 1960; the UN intervened in Zaire for
years; this is very well recounted in Brian Urquhart's book on Ralph
Bunche, which reminds one that there is nothing new under the sun
and that the UN went through a great deal of turbulence in that
case, which involved both issues of internal governance and a problem of secession (of Katanga, the richest province). As I said in the
first lecture, UN intervention is deemed legitimate when the civil
war is seen as threatening international peace and security. This is
what the Europeans and the Security Council decided in the case
of Yugoslavia. But such intervention has to be guided by the principle of impartiality. The UN tried very hard in the Congo case to

remain impartial; at some moments this turned out to be quite impossible. But the policy that Hammarskjöld tried to follow, as long as he lived, was at least a façade of impartiality among the various factions which were then fighting for control of the former Belgian colony. This has also been the UN stance in Yugoslavia. On the other hand, if the war is seen as an international conflict—and indeed we have now a recognized sovereign state of Croatia, a recognized state of Bosnia-Herzegovina, and a state of Yugoslavia—and if the armed forces of one country, Serbia, are found to have crossed the borders of the others, certainly that does not rule out, for the UN or for the Europeans, a possible attempt at being neutral. After all, the way in which the UN had handled the India-Pakistan wars in the past was to try to remain impartial; similarly, in the Middle East. But in an international conflict it can also become possible, and sometimes indeed necessary, for third parties to proclaim that one of the belligerents has committed aggression against the others, that one cannot remain impartial between the aggressor and the victim, and that the various provisions of the Charter that deal with aggression have to be applied.

The reality in the case of Yugoslavia was clearly a mix of both. There are large elements of civil war; certainly the Serbs in Croatia moved on their own to proclaim a separate republic, and the Serbs in Bosnia did the same thing in April 1992. However, in both cases they were armed by the Serbs from Serbia, and the Serbian army intervened and provided much of the military might without which the Serbs in those two places could not have occupied as much ground as they did. In other words, it was Serbia which crossed what were now internationally recognized borders and kept the war going. Without Serb support, the Bosnian Serbs could not have continued to fight and advance, even after the pro forma split between Milosevic in Belgrade and Karadzic in Pale.

The third question is, What would the international community do if it did organize a collective intervention? Whether it is the European Community or the UN, what would it intervene for? What is the priority? Here we find a conflict of priorities. One possible line is that priority ought to be given to a peaceful settlement of the dispute, whether it takes the form of a reconstituted loose confederation of Yugoslavia, as many hoped in the beginning, or of a peace treaty between Serbia and its independent neighbors which finally settles the borders and guarantees certain kinds of rights to minorities. But anyhow, a negotiated settlement which would bring back peace could be the chief objective, because it is clear that cease-fires that are not tied to a peaceful settlement do not last very long. This could be called the settlement option.

The other possibility would have given priority to helping the victim. If we look at Bosnia as a case of aggression, the priority, as in the case of the Gulf war, must be helping the victim. The victims of aggression under the UN Charter have an inherent right of self-defense, which means among other things that they are entitled to receive arms. This also would have meant imposing sanctions, economic or military, against Serbia. Some sanctions—economic—were imposed on the Serbs. But an arms embargo was applied to all par-ties—a decision that in fact helped the well-armed Serbs. The argu-ment was that if one goes too far in the direction of treating this as a case of aggression, coming to the help of the victim might make the war fiercer and a peaceful settlement more difficult. And so we have had both endless attempts at a negotiated solution, and very limited, rather toothless attempts to protect the victims of aggres-sion, such as safe havens and no-fly zones. The main effort has con-sisted in treating the Yugoslav disaster primarily as a case of hu-manitarian intervention, especially in Bosnia, where UNPROFOR was sent on a humanitarian mission to provide relief and food for the inhabitants of Sarajevo and other isolated places. This was a way of fudging the distinction between the diplomatic objective of a settlement which would have required treating the parties pretty much as moral (or immoral) equals, and the notion of aggression, in which the victims have to be helped not only by food and relief convoys but also by military and diplomatic support.

We now come to the problem of international confusion. It is a very sad story. At first, the European Community let it be known that this affair was going to be its baby, and indeed told the Ameri-cans that it did not particularly want them or NATO to get in-volved—which suited the Bush administration very well indeed. At first, then, there was a short wave of Brussels enthusiasm: let us do this, it is taking place in Europe, we Europeans have been talking about defining a common foreign and defense policy, so we have a great opportunity to try and resolve the issue. The first negotiator for the Community was Lord Carrington, the former Secretary General of NATO and former British Foreign Minister; he negotiated with the parties, Serbia and Croatia, for several months. In October 1991 he came up with a very interesting plan, essentially an attempt at setting up a loose confederation, granting very extensive minority rights to the Serbs who would have been in the non-Serbian parts of the confederation, and granting a special status to the Albanians in Serbia's Kosovo.

That plan was rejected by the Serbs. This discouraged Lord Carrington, who went home, and it led the European Community's foreign ministers to dump the case on others. The United States made some polite noises about how NATO might look into the matter, but it did not really press the case very much. The French, needless to say, did not want NATO. This was at a time when the theological war which had been going on forever between the U.S. and the French about the role of NATO was blazing (the Clinton Administration has not had quite the same ideological fervor as the Bush team about the supremacy of NATO). The French did not want the Americans to expand the geographical reach of NATO, so the issue was referred to the UN Security Council.

In the case of Croatia, the Security Council presided over the cease-fire agreement which was finally achieved in January 1992. The agreement left a very large part of Croatia in Serbian hands, in particular the whole Krajina (the eastern part of Croatia), and sent the United Nations (UNPROFOR) force as a peace-keeping force into the Serbian-occupied territory, with a very ambitious mission to disarm the parties and oversee the dismantling of weapons. It was never able to carry out that mission, and when fighting resumed UNPROFOR was simply pushed aside.

When it became clear that there was a serious risk of war in Bosnia, the Security Council said that the situation constituted a threat to peace, but it could do nothing to prevent a war which has led to massive ethnic cleansing and flights of refugees, to the siege and shelling of a number of cities. In the case of Bosnia, UNPROFOR was sent neither as a peacekeeping unit, because there was no cease-fire agreement, nor as a force allowed to use its arms to protect the victims of Serb attacks, but merely as a humanitarian operation.

What did the Security Council do beyond this? In a sense, it fell between two stools. On the whole it gave priority to what I call the settlement option, which requires, as I said a little earlier, that the parties be treated more or less equally; because of this, one plan after the other has been negotiated in vain: first by Cyrus Vance and Lord Owen, later when Mr. Vance got fed up, by Mr. Stoltenberg and Lord Owen, now by Stoltenberg and Carl Bildt. Each plan yielded a little bit more ground to the Serbs, which is inevitable if one treats the parties equally and if one of the parties, being stronger than the other, produces its own "realities" on the ground by superior military force. On the other hand, timidly and largely because of the rather blatant nature of Serb actions, the Security Council took a few measures that looked as if they were based on the model of aggression and were aimed at helping the victim. "Safe" areas were designated—but at no point was any attempt made to get the Serbs to lift their siege of Sarajevo, a siege that brought death to thousands of civilians and seriously damaged the UN's humanitarian deliveries. Of the two most significant measures aimed at the Serbs, the first was the authority given to UN forces in Bosnia to resort to force, or rather to ask NATO to resort to force since one cannot ask humanitarian people to use it themselves, but only under very limited conditions. It was authorized not in order to protect the Bosnians, not even in the "safe areas," from attack but in order to protect the UN force, if UNPROFOR came under attack. This, of course, was one of the reasons why the few actual resorts to force were not much more than pinpricks, almost like a ritual, in which the UN or NATO actually warned the Serbs in advance which targets would be bombed: a remarkable form of chivalry which shows a bizarre confusion between the need to be nice to the Serbs because one wanted to reach an agreement with them, and the idea of protecting the victims from Serbian aggressions. One was trying to sit on both stools at the same time.

The second way in which the Security Council tried to do something for the victims has been the setting-up of an International Criminal Tribunal, a very interesting experiment, the first since Nuremberg. The UN has never succeeded in establishing an international tribunal with a global scope, so here there was an element of progress. But once again, as in the case of authorized uses of force, this tribunal was set up in conditions which have led some people to suspect that it was no more than a moral alibi, allowing those who set it up to have a good conscience, rather than a genuine effort to deal with the massive crimes that have been committed. How else can one explain the very small budget of the tribunal, its very limited resources both financial and in terms of personnel—even though such a tribunal would need a whole network of people capable of investigating charges, of finding the witnesses and getting them to talk (many of the witnesses are quite unwilling to talk because they are afraid of the consequences). The tribunal does not really have the means to fully carry out its mandate.

There is also the provision that it cannot judge criminals in absentia, and then, of course, it faces the key problem: how do you *get* the people that you want to indict? You can indict them in absentia, but you cannot judge them. The tribunal is entirely dependent on either some of those war criminals making the bad mistake of going to a country like Germany on vacation and being arrested by the Germans, or else on the goodwill of Mr. Milosevic or Mr. Karadzic, two gentlemen who are not known for their altruism, and whose willingness to deliver to the international tribunal some of those criminals is pretty questionable. Since the tribunal made it fairly clear that it did not want to go after only the small fry, but wanted to go after the really big fish, those who ordered rapes and massacres which are of an almost unbelievably horrendous nature—it has indicted Karadzic and General Mladic, the Bosnian Serb commander—it is quite unlikely that these gentlemen are going to deliver top commanders, heads of concentration camps, or themselves. And it is also very clear, when one talks both with UN officials and with government representatives (you will not find this in print), that they basically consider the tribunal to be a nuisance, an obstacle to a settlement, because, needless to say, the Serbs do not like it. If

only the parties could reach a settlement which would grant amnesty to all the criminals and make the tribunal unnecessary, many
would be much relieved.

Of course, if one wants a settlement, since everything at this
point depends on the Serbs both in Belgrade and in Pale, not an-
noying the Serbs becomes a prerequisite. The whole operation is
torn between the fact that it is the Serbs who are very largely (certainly, in the case of Bosnia) responsible for much of what has been
happening, and the need of being nice to the Serbs not only in order
to reach an agreement, which the Bosnian Serbs are holding up, but
also because if the Serbs are not nice UNPROFOR is in trouble.
This has been the problem throughout. Technically, the UN has
operated between two stools. It has been reluctant to call this a case
of collective security under Chapter VII, largely because it was
afraid of the implications. If it is a case of collective security, one
would have to take costly and extensive measures; how far would
one have to go beyond pinprick air strikes, even beyond much larger
air strikes? If these do not suffice, one may need an abundance of
troops that nobody has been willing to provide. The maintenance
of UNPROFOR is being "justified" by reference to its humanitarian
mission, which, thanks to Serb misdeeds ranging from road block-
ades to the creation of new humanitarian disasters, it is increasingly
incapable of carrying out. The real justification is the refusal to fight
the Serbs: and as long as UNPROFOR is there, its hostage nature
deters, not of course the Serbs, but those who would like to confront them by force. Above all the very existence of UNPROFOR
has become a strong argument against treating this as a case of collective security because UNPROFOR is, in fact, a hostage whom the
Serbs can squeeze whenever they like—pushing it around, blocking
its mission, taking its members hostages. So we have had to witness
this extraordinarily sad case of humanitarian intervention which ob-
jectively helps the aggressor—if one looks at this as a case of aggression. The Americans are reluctant to provide any ground troops
at all (except for extrication, paradoxically—indeed doubly paradoxically since a retreat might be very risky); and those states that
have sent forces to UNPROFOR do not want them to fight the
Serbs, except in self-defense, interpreted as narrowly as possible. And

so, the fall of the "safe area" of Srebrenica saw UN forces seized by the Serbs, who thus deterred air strikes, and UN soldiers passively witnessing the massacre of civilians.

These paradoxes explain a bizarre series of events: first, those negotiations and their evanescent outcomes, the various plans—plan 1, plan 2; then the Stoltenberg plan, and then the contact group plan. All were negotiated without the UN, or the negotiators for the UN and the European Community, ever using a threat of force with the Serbs in order to push them toward accepting a settlement. It is not the best way of negotiating. In any case, when you come to the party that is winning on the ground and say, "Look, if you are not reasonable there is nothing I will do to you," failure is preordained. I was very much struck, having often listened on television to Lord Owen at the time he was negotiating the first plan—he is a very eloquent man—by his saying that nothing could disturb the negotiations more than a threat to force, for that would annoy the parties, or rather the one party that would have been the target of the use of force, meaning the Serbs. A few months later when the Owen-Vance plan was definitely buried, he wrote in an article in *Foreign Affairs* that the whole idea of negotiating without using the threat of force was, of course, preposterous in the first place. But it took him until his plan had failed to realize something which any vaguely intelligent student of diplomacy could have told him in the beginning. There was one moment in particular when a threat of resorting to force might have been highly effective; this was the bombing of Dubrovnik by the Serbs during the war with Croatia in December 1991. The commander of NATO in Europe called on the Chairman of the Joint Chiefs of Staff in Washington, General Powell, and suggested that there be a raid against the Serbs because NATO had a fleet and planes were ready. General Powell allegedly said, "We do deserts, we don't do mountains." He checked with his superiors in the Bush administration, who decided that this was not the moment or the place for military engagement—and so the moment passed and there was no resort to force (except, a few days later, in Somalia, which was wrongly seen as practically fail-safe). Later, there were a few threats throughout 1993 and 1994 to halfheartedly protect safe zones. These pinpricks were so limited that they never amounted to very much. The handful of bombs dropped around Pale in May 1995 proved not only ineffective but disastrous: it allowed the Serbs to take hundreds of UNPROFOR members as hostages, and led the UN and NATO to stop enforcing the heavy weapons exclusion in the Sarajevo area, and to stop threatening further bombings. In addition, even though economic sanctions were imposed on the Serbs, they have been treated less as a form of punishment against aggression than as a bargaining chip with the Serbs.

The truth is that the UN has put most of its emphasis on the goal of getting a settlement at almost any costs. The idea that an internationally brokered settlement should not reward aggression and ethnic cleansing or dismantle the state that has been attacked appears to have been quietly shelved as "unrealistic." The embargo on arms for Bosnia has been maintained (although one can argue that it violates the Charter's emphasis on the inherent right of self-defense) because an escalation of the war could lead to an East-West crisis, and because it would make a settlement more difficult. Each time someone has suggested something much more forceful there has been an outcry: if one resorts to force, for instance some time ago in Bihac, this will compromise the achievement of a peace settlement, as if there had been a peace settlement on the verge of being achieved. The result is that the restoration of peace has been entirely at the mercy of events on the battlefield. Each plan, although it left a little bit more of Bosnia in Serb hands, ended up being rejected if not by Serbia, then by the Bosnian Serbs; so everything ended up at the mercy of Serbian goodwill. There would have been a very strong case, in the abstract, for a different sort of strategy, which I understand had been proposed by at least one American Secretary of Defense, Les Aspin. He wanted the UN or the Europeans to concentrate first on the end of violence—in other words to impose a cease-fire by force if necessary, so that the seizing of territory by Serbian force and the attendant human rights violations would have to cease. The diplomatic negotiations would have occurred only after the cease-fire and an end of those violations. Instead, we have negotiated during an endless war, which has meant more violations of human rights, and which, partly because of the imbalance in armaments, always gave the bargaining advantage to the Serbs. Why was this alternative not selected? After all, this was how many of the Middle Eastern crises had been handled; the first imperative is to obtain a cease-fire, and then one can negotiate, but one should not do both at the same time.

The explanation is obvious: this was a case where all of the obstacles to collective intervention I described in the first lecture could be found, and the most important was the absence of any will to do more than drift. When one wants to drift, it is wonderful to be able to say: we have a great humanitarian operation thanks to which the inhabitants of Sarajevo can be fed (so that they can then be picked out by one sniper after the other while they line up for food and water), and it is wonderful that we have a peace negotiation going on permanently with all the parties.

The United States has condemned itself to impotence from the beginning by the very firm decision which was reached by the Bush administration (and of course, was clearly maintained by Clinton despite his campaign criticism of it) not to put forces on the ground under any circumstances and not to engage in any large scale naval or air action that could then lead to the use of ground forces. There is no immediate connection between buzzing or even bombing one particular corner of a Serbian airport which has been cleared of all aircraft because one warned the Serbs first, and sending ground forces. But massive air attacks which would not have succeeded in stopping Bosnian Serb attacks might then lead to the next step, ground forces. The U.S. decided from the beginning that this was not a rewarding terrain, and that American security interests were not at stake; the key security interest was defined as containing the war (a good reason against using force), and the idea that there may be equally important "world order" interests was not treated seriously. This has put the U.S. in an extraordinarily disagreeable position. First, it said nothing—that is pretty much what happened throughout the year 1992, when George Bush was still in power; it left the Europeans handling the crisis along with Mr. Vance as representative of the UN, and Owen and Vance were no match for the Serbs. When Clinton started telling his European allies that they were too meek and too mild and too appeasement-like, the Europeans could answer, Who are you to give us advice? We at least have troops in an exposed position, you are just criticizing us without wanting to commit any forces whatsoever; put up or shut up. This is the friendly dialogue which has been going on pretty much throughout the Clinton administration. What made it change its stance late in the summer of 1995 was that the alternative to a resort to force aimed at a genuine cease-fire and embryonic settlement was far worse: an American military intervention aimed at helping UNPROFOR extricate itself ignominiously from a war-ravaged Bosnia.

Germany was the one state that from the beginning wanted to look at Serbia as the aggressor. Germany has a very large contingent of Croatian workers on its soil, especially in conservative Bavaria; the German Christian Democratic Party in Bavaria (CSU) was very sympathetic to them. Germany, having achieved its unification through the application of the principle of self-determination, had genuine sympathy for the demands of the Croats and the Slovenes and later the Bosnians; and, needless to say, historically the Germans had never had particular sympathies for the Serbs. It is very interesting that my good friend Josef Joffe, a leading German writer on world affairs and a Jew whose family was annihilated by the Nazis— certainly not your average conservative German—put the blame, when he started writing articles on Yugoslavia in the *Süddeutsche Zeitung* as editor-in-chief, not only for the current drama but for the outbreak of World War One on Serbia. Germany, from the beginning, for good reasons and for historical reasons (historical reasons are not necessarily good ones), had its sympathies clearly marked. But while the Germans could denounce the Serbs for all sorts of reasons, Germany could not do much except bully its allies into recognizing Croatia and Slovenia, because of the constitutional limitations which prevent Germany from sending forces to fight outside. Once the German government realized that there was something slightly ridiculous in taking this very exposed diplomatic position but being unable to back it with force, and once it saw that recognition had not had the deterrent effect on Serbia which it quite wrongly expected, it just went silent and has not really played any major role since.

The British and the French—the British with great consistency

and the French with a greater rhetorical tendency to play Hamlet—
have since the beginning made it very clear that their purpose was
a negotiated settlement, and that this was not a problem that could
be solved by the use of outside force. The result was that each time
the Clinton administration, in particular, advocated a resort to more
extensive threats to use outside force, or either Clinton or, later, the
U.S. Congress, advocated lifting the arms embargo on Bosnia, the
British and the French said they would take their own contingents
out of UNPROFOR in such a case. So there was a sort of blackmail
exerted by the British and the French on the Americans, who were
only too easy to blackmail because they have a fairly bad conscience
about not being on the ground. Each time there was a particularly
obnoxious Serbian action, such as an intrusion in a so-called safe
area, the Americans would say, we really have to do something, and
the British and the French would say, if you try to do that, we take
UNPROFOR out and these poor people will starve. What explains
this curious policy?

It is very hard to get to the root of it. In the British case it seems
to me (this may be unfair) that there is more than a little bit of the
Chamberlain attitude—far away people about whom we don't want
to know more than we already know—a sort of conviction that the
Balkans are a witch's brew, and therefore let us not get involved too
deeply. This is very much the attitude that George Kennan has in
this country (I am referring to a piece he wrote a couple of years
ago as an introduction to a pre-World War One Carnegie Endowment report on the Balkans). Kennan argued that these people are
not like us; we are civilized, they have always been more savage, and
therefore there is nothing we can do except express regret and com-
passion.

In the French case there has been a much stronger component
of sympathy for Serbia, especially among the military. After all, Serbia is an old French ally. On the ground, some of the military, both
British and French, often have had a tendency of looking at the
Serbian army as a genuine army whereas the Bosnians are barely
armed amateurs, not well organized as a fighting force. There is a
certain amount of military professionalism here. French opinion has
been divided. Many intellectuals have been actively campaigning for

a more overtly pro-Bosnian policy, on grounds of human rights and self-determination. But one also often hears the argument: do you really want a Muslim state in Europe? (Those who make it do not seem to realize that one thing that is likely to turn this largely secular Muslim people into Islamists is treating them as canon fodder for the Serbs.) One may not see that argument very much in print, but one hears it in colloquia, debates, and conversations. What appears to have changed the French position at last in the summer of 1995 is the election of President Chirac, who appears fed up less by the treatment of the Muslims by the Bosnian Serbs than by the humiliation of UNPROFOR at Bosnian Serb hands. But here comes a new paradox: a possible French pullout, not, as before, if NATO is used, but if American fears of engagement and British policy prevent, despite the fine words that followed the fall of two "safe areas" in July 1995, any toughening of UNPROFOR's mission or any retaliation for Bosnian Serb attacks on that mission—and also, as before, if the U.S. decided to lift the arms embargo on Bosnia.

As for Russia, of course, by the time it got involved in the Bosnian affair it was very much on the side of Serbia, for grand historical reasons. Thus Russia has also leaned in the direction of opposing UN uses of force. The consequence of the collective absence of will has been the organizational fiasco which many commentators have described. It is true that the chain of command is slightly preposterous. It goes from the Security Council (which has voted countless resolutions that cannot be enforced) to Mr. Boutros-Ghali, to his meek Japanese representative on the ground (a great believer in consensus), to the commander of the UN forces in Bosnia who is primarily concerned with protecting UNPROFOR, and from there to NATO: a very complicated chain of command, with recurrent tensions between every two elements of it. Much of the press commentary has tended to blame this extraordinary set of hurdles for the fiasco.

However, in the Gulf War the chain of command was exactly as complicated, in fact even more so. In addition to the UN and NATO there was the West European Union (whose role in Yugoslavia is minimal), yet it worked like clockwork. The reasons are very simple: there was one power, the U.S., which was calling the shots, and there was a broad international consensus. So what could have become hurdles disappeared. In this case, since there is no will or leadership, everything that could go wrong, went wrong.

To conclude: an absolutely disastrous precedent has been set. It is the precedent that you can impose your will through unbelievable atrocities and get away with it. Given the fact that in much of the world, including all of the former Soviet Union (and especially the Caucasus), situations exist which look very much like the situation in Yugoslavia, cases where there are minorities at odds with ethnic or religious majorities or with other minorities, the precedent set here is an extraordinary invitation to settle those kinds of issues by brute force. The destruction of a multi-ethnic entity by one ethnic group's violence is another abject aspect of this fiasco. Finally, the Yugoslav case confirms all of the difficulties of collective interventions when domestic and international aspects mix, in instances which are not dealt with as clear-cut cases of collective security. If there is neither peace to keep nor power behind a mere peacekeeping force, as was the case here, not only will it have trouble carrying out its humanitarian purposes, but it can actually become an obstacle rather than a contribution to a settlement. Today, it contributes very little to order, and nothing at all (on the contrary) to justice. What this shows is that it is necessary to create the conditions which will make a return to peace—and a just peace—possible. This may require, in a case like Yugoslavia, a resort to force on the part of the international community. It may, in other cases like Somalia and Haiti, involve very deep domestic reforms, and when the outside powers are very reluctant to go so far, the result is something of a mess. A last lesson concerns the limits of humanitarian action. As long as the factors that led to humanitarian nightmares—massacres, refugees, starvation—are not properly and promptly addressed, as the criminal acts that cause them are allowed to go on, and there is neither peace nor a fair settlement of the issues, humanitarian efforts are doomed, at best, to imitate Sisyphus, and at worst to remind us that the road to hell is paved with good intentions.

After this fiasco, which adds itself to a number of others, the trend will be, at best, a tendency to license a regional great power to clean up the mess around its borders, for instance, licensing Rus-

sia to act as a hegemon in areas like Georgia; or else, as was again
the case in the Chechnian crisis, it will be a tendency to do nothing
and to look the other way. The Dayton agreements of November
1995 are so riddled with contradictions and have—for all the reasons
shown in this essay—proved so difficult to enforce that peace remains fragile, and justice pushed aside. But there is one thing this
debacle demonstrates, and that is the strength of the argument that
was made by Adam Roberts: if one separates the purely humanitarian aspects from the political factors that led to the humanitarian
disaster and, in addition to this, if one treats massive violations of
human rights as if they were the equivalent of a famine or an earth-
quake or a flood, one simply closes one's eyes on the realities. This
is what everyone has done, so as to be able to concentrate on domestic politics and to preserve a narrow and shortsighted definition
of national security and national interest.

Final Thoughts

This section is being written eight months after the Dayton
agreements. They have succeeded, for the first time, in putting an
end to armed conflict and atrocities. But the Yugoslav tragedy is not
over.

In retrospect, there was probably no way of preventing a bloody
disintegration of the Yugoslav Federation. In the "infernal triangle"
of sovereignty, self-determination, and human rights, there were
only bad choices. Self-determination for each ethnic community
would have resulted in a greater Serbia that Croatia was not willing
to tolerate and that would have dismembered Bosnia. Human rights
for minorities were not likely to be respected as long as the dominant
ethnic group saw the others as enemies to be expelled or annihilated. Sovereignty was a profoundly ambiguous and unsatisfactory
norm: ambiguous, because it could mean either the preservation of
the former Yugoslavia, which Slovenia and Croatia rejected, or the
secession of existing administrative units such as Slovenia, Croatia,
and Bosnia; but the latter—which was endorsed by the European
Union and the international society—was unsatisfactory because of

the unwillingness of Croat and Serb minorities in Bosnia and of Serb minorities in Croatia to accept "foreign" rule. As a result, sovereignty could not fulfill its main function—to protect the population of the "sovereign" state. An agreement that would have allowed for the transformation of the Yugoslav Federation into a loose confederation, or for the creation of successor states each one of which was willing to enforce the kinds of rights for minorities (tantamount to autonomy) requested by the Badinter Commission, would have represented an accommodation among the three sides of the triangle. But it was never in the cards, and has still not been achieved. Croatia's respect for minority rights (indeed, for the rights of political opposition) is questionable, and the future of Bosnia remains in doubt.

The long war in Bosnia showed the limits of humanitarian intervention in two different ways. First, when atrocities reach a certain level—as has also been the case in Rwanda, and, it seems, will be the case in Burundi, the humanitarian organizations, public and private, that try to protect the victims and provide food and medical care are all too easily overwhelmed by the magnitude of the task. The international society is badly equipped to cope with genocide and ethnic cleansing. Secondly, putting an end to such horrors so that the number of victims ceases to rise and the survivors begin to feel safe requires more than the minimal uses of force authorized by the Security Council in Bosnia before August 1995—uses that provided only potection for UNPROFOR from direct attack but, as in Srebrenica, left the UN impotent and the victims at the mercy of the killers. For the problem is not just to enforce humanitarian operations; it is to put an end to the violence that makes such operations both necessary and to some extent futile, or at least Sisyphean. There can be such a resort to force only if the international society is willing to designate the aggressor rather than treating victims and victimizers alike, and if the powers that have the necessary military might are willing to use it.

This was clearly demonstrated in the spring and summer of 1995, when the United States, having allowed Croatia to acquire weapons (including from Iran) and helped it train for their use, encouraged the Croat army to reconquer Krajina, and the Croats and Bosnians to regain enough land to limit the Bosnian Serbs to the 49 percent of Bosnia that the latest contact group plan had allocated to them. It was demonstrated decisively when, after one more murderous shelling of Sarajevo, NATO's air strikes, after months of mere symbolic actions, pounded Bosnian Serbs into submission. The United States, as we know, had been hesitating for years between moral indignation without teeth, aimed at the Bosnian Serbs, and—especially after Somalia—a fear of casualties, a desire for combatant immunity extraordinary for the world's superpower. America's main European allies were either, like Germany, constitutionally incapacitated or, like Britain and France, afraid of the quagmire and reluctant to condemn and punish one side in the conflict. The American position changed only when the Clinton administration had its back to the wall; the credibility of NATO was at stake, and a withdrawal of UNPROFOR would have been both a disgrace and a source of American casualties, since U.S. forces would have been needed for extrication. At home such a debacle would have been a godsend for Republicans. Hence the NATO shift to real force, and Richard Holbrooke's blitz.

But the old oscillation between treating Serbia (not merely the Bosnian Serbs, whom Milosevic at least partly controls if only through general Mladic) as an aggressor, and treating the parties as morally equivalent, has not disappeared. The Dayton agreements are a shaky compromise between these two tendencies. This is why these documents are more likely to resemble, at the end, the U.S.-North Vietnam agreement of January 1973 than the historic achievement celebrated by Holbrooke. They may merely provide a "decent interval" before the partition of Bosnia.

At the very core of Dayton, we find a contradiction between the establishment of at least two separate entities (the very shaky Croat-Bosnian Federation and the Serb Republic) and the principle of a unified (if decentralized) multi-ethnic state of Bosnia. The role of IFOR has been at the same time effective and counterproductive: effective in ensuring peace and a separation of forces, counterproductive not only insofar as military separation strengthens ethnic separation, but above all because the fear of mission creep and of American casualties has led NATO's commanders to do nothing to promote the return of refugees—provided for at Dayton—that might have partly undone ethnic cleansing. They have also refused to arrest war criminals by hiding behind the words of the Dayton accord (carefully crafted to soothe the Serbs), which entrust the delivery of these criminals to international justic to the respective parties—a guarantee of fiasco! This minimalism of IFOR reflects a return to what had been the main pattern of the Bosnian war. For a brief moment in the middle of 1995, Chirac's France and Clinton jointly decided that the time for toughness had come; after Dayton, French preferences for "diplomatic" methods, French and British doubts about the Hague tribunal (seen as an obstacle to peace and reconciliation—as if there could be reconciliation without justice— as well as dubious precedent) and America's fear of entrapment have all converged.

It is difficult to interpret Dayton as being more than a construction aimed at giving the Clinton administration a "victory" that would last until the 1996 election—whatever happens afterward— and aimed at allowing it to withdraw most if not all of its forces by the end of 1996. Hence the push for elections, even though the conditions for fair competition among parties have clearly not been created; the elections will formally allow IFOR to declare that its main mission is over. But they are likely to lead to the triumph of ethnic and separatist parties, and to be one more step toward a partition of Bosnia. The contrast between the single-minded, narrow efficiency of IFOR, and the confusing proliferation of agencies in charge of civilian reconstruction, under the somewhat nonchalant supervision of Carl Bildt, confirms this interpretation. And the recent "agreement" between Milosevic and Holbrooke in July 1996, about the removal of Karadzic from positions of power, has a sour taste. It does nothing to remove him from influence over his subordinates and nothing to bring him to justice.

The worst is not always sure to happen; the worst would be a resumption of hostilities, say, if the Serb Republic decides to rejoin Serbia, and the Bosnian government decides to fight; or if Croats and Serbs fight over Eastern Slavonia. But the alternative seems to be a partition that ratifies ethnic cleansing and mass atrocities: a conclusion that may be "realistic" but is morally repugnant.

NOTE

1. See in particular Susan L. Woodward, *Balkan Tragedy* (Washington, D.C.: Brookings Institution, 1995); David Reiff, *Slaughterhouse* (New York: Simon and Schuster, 1994); Henry Wynaendts, *L'engrenage* (Paris: Denoël, 1993).

4

LIMITS AND OPPORTUNITIES IN HUMANITARIAN INTERVENTION

Robert C. Johansen

STANLEY HOFFMANN ARGUES convincingly, first of all, that humanitarian intervention is fraught with so many dangers of abuse and difficulties in execution that the international community should proceed with utmost caution as it expands the instances where it may be practiced. Indeed, readers might be a bit surprised that he wants to open the door to additional interventions at all, given his long and persuasive litany of reasons why states are reluctant to accept the risks and costs of military interventions, or, if they do intervene, why such interventions either may not uphold high normative standards or succeed in practice. The calamities of United Nations efforts in Somalia and Bosnia illustrate the moral, military, and political difficulties. Despite the difficulties, however, Hoffmann believes, secondly, that to refuse to intervene at all is morally unacceptable in cases where gross violations of human rights occur and that to rule out humanitarian intervention completely would encourage unilateral interventions, which are more inclined to abuse than multilaterally administered interventions. These two central themes live in tension with each other, as Hoffmann acknowledges.

In commenting upon his stimulating analysis, I will advance the thesis that scholars and the international community should give more emphasis to finding a third path between doing nothing and sending in the troops. This path should include instruments that are nonmilitary yet still coercive. Indeed, international measures that aim at "less" than deploying military forces may, in the end, yield better results in deterring human rights violations. As the European and UN inability to halt ethnic "cleansing" during three years of fighting in Bosnia demonstrates, the problem with focusing on military instruments is twofold: the severe difficulties attending their use may make them ineffective, and the military focus interferes with taking nonmilitary measures seriously. Furthermore, as the UN attempt—and failure—to apprehend warring clan leaders in Somalia reminds us, even when the UN takes military action, difficulties often lead to erosion of mission legitimacy, loss of political and financial support, and failure to achieve intended goals. In short, in some cases the use of military force, even under UN auspices, may accomplish fewer normative benefits than could carefully planned and orchestrated nonmilitary measures.[1] This possibility suggests the merit in giving more emphasis to nonmilitary instruments, some of which could still be coercive, even though states will be unlikely to exclude military means completely. The presumption against military intervention in this essay is not based, as it often has been in the past, on the principle of inviolable sovereignty. It is based instead on the demonstrated high costs and low utility of military intervention in addressing underlying causes of humanitarian disasters.

1. The Need for Conceptual Clarity

Before discussing proposed guidelines for future humanitarian interventions, we should clarify the meaning of humanitarian intervention. Despite his focus on the concept, Hoffmann has failed to provide a strict definition of it. This weakens the power of his analysis, because he occasionally slips back and forth in using the two quite different concepts of (1) collective security against aggression and (2) humanitarian intervention, as if they were interchangeable or at least not clearly differentiated. Indeed, his writing blurs distinctions by occasionally employing a linguistic hybrid of the two concepts in referring to "collective intervention." For example, in summarizing his position, Hoffmann writes: "Our 'universal maxim' has already been stated: it allows for collective intervention when a state's condition or behavior results in grave threats to other states' and peoples' peace and security, and in grave and massive violations of human rights."[2] But the first of his two triggering conditions in this maxim for intervention, "grave threats to . . . peace," may have little or nothing to do with humanitarian intervention. It refers to threats to the peace that will justify international action under Chapter VII of the UN Charter, including whatever collective security measures the Security Council decides to muster. Similarly, Hoffmann indicates that one of two *Grundnormen* on which his doctrine of humanitarian intervention rests is "the right of states and people to peace and security."[3] Again, any threat to the peace would trigger Chapter VII actions that are not subject to the usual constraints on humanitarian intervention.

Hoffmann's analysis implicitly reinforces the recent Security Council inclination to justify intervention with arguments simultaneously drawn both from human rights concerns and the Council's obligation to protect peace and security. The Council prefers to stretch the meaning of peace and security to cover interventions that may be prompted mainly by human rights violations because the Charter is very clear that the Council's powers are virtually unlimited in the area of peace and security, but interventions for other reasons have traditionally been limited by the principle of nonintervention in a sovereign member's domestic jurisdiction. As the Charter declares in Article 2(7), "Nothing contained in the present Charter shall authorize the United Nations to intervene in matters which are essentially within the domestic jurisdiction of any state. . . . " The Charter makes no reference to the use of force for humanitarian purposes. Although there are good human rights reasons for finding appropriate rationales and means for intervening in more humanitarian cases today than in the past, several problems could arise in blurring the line between interventions justified for (1) maintaining international peace and security and (2) halting gross violations of human rights. The contemporary normative task is to expand carefully the space for legitimate intervention on human rights grounds, without basing the rationale for intervention primarily on the idea that gross violations of human rights constitute a threat to the peace, because such a rationale could cause confusion about mandates, the nature of military deployments, rules of engagement, and reasons for offering or denying political support.[4]

First, collective security and humanitarian intervention should be kept analytically separate because the reservations about violating the principle of nonintervention and penetrating a country's sovereignty simply do not apply when considering collective security actions to maintain peace. If a government commits aggression and the Security Council acts against it, inhibitions about encroaching on domestic jurisdiction are suspended. As Article 2(7) of the Charter clearly states, "this [domestic jurisdiction] principle shall not prejudice the application of enforcement measures under Chapter VII." Indeed, if the Security Council determines that a government's external policies or even its *internal* policies constitute a threat to international peace, then action against that state may be taken without the international community being constrained by the nonintervention principle. On the other hand, when the target of possible intervention has *not* flouted the norms against aggression but *has* violated fundamental human rights, then the non-intervention test of Article 2(7) poses cautionary limits on collective action. Presumably, external intervention in such a case should be minimized and carefully calibrated so as not to exceed what is necessary to end the specific human rights violation that prompted intervention in the first place.

Second, failure to distinguish between humanitarian intervention against violations of human rights, which threaten a humane domestic society, and collective security action against aggression, which threatens the international order, could make reluctance to intervene against violations of human rights appear to be more dangerous, consequential, and likely to threaten international order than is warranted. Of course by ruling out references to the Munich analogy and appeasement of aggression, since these apply only to collective security issues, one also removes a popular rationale for justifying humanitarian intervention. Nonetheless, clear differentiation of the concepts helps avoid the dangerous tendency to justify humanitarian intervention by appealing (falsely) to people's sense of the need to resist aggression. On the other hand, to win support for opposing breaches of the peace, the UN does not need to fall back upon the arguments required to justify humanitarian intervention because in such cases the Security Council is legally entitled to take any action it would like without the domestic jurisdiction principle of Article 2(7) coming into play.

Third, intellectual imprecision in blending these concepts strikingly parallels and could unwisely encourage the traditional tendency of powerful states to justify their own unwarranted intervention in another state's domestic jurisdiction by claiming such intervention is necessary to protect international peace and security. For example, in drawing lessons for humanitarian intervention from his comments on the UN chain of command in the Gulf War,[5] which was really a collective response to military aggression, and the "Chamberlain attitude" of the British,[6] which was really a case of appeasing military aggression, the author may unintentionally obscure the need to understand humanitarian intervention as a distinct form of multilateral action.

If humanitarian intervention is conflated with threats to the peace and self-defense against aggression, it could tempt great powers to intervene for self-interested reasons, using human rights and vague threats to the peace as a pretense, even though no armed attack has occurred, the singular condition allowing unilateral acts of self-defense under Article 51 of the Charter.[7] This danger is especially serious and destablizing if *unilateral* intervention is allowed. Although Hoffmann prefers authorization by the UN or a regional organization, he does recommend that unilateral intervention be allowed when the UN is "incapable of dealing with . . . an issue."[8] Such a vague loophole is dangerous enough when a strict understanding of humanitarian intervention is in vogue. Imagine what pernicious use can be made of that exception to the need for UN authorization when humanitarian intervention is imprecisely thought to cover threats to peace. Any government alleging some threatening policy by an adversary could claim it was justified in unilateral military intervention.

Fourth, in addition to the danger that an undifferentiated concept of intervention could be subject to abuse by powerful states, it also could increase opposition from the weak—opposition that would be less likely with a more strict understanding of humanitarian intervention. Of course, weak states are unenthusiastic about intervention in the first place, because it usually occurs against them, not against the powerful. But if small, medium, and great powers would make clear that humanitarian intervention could be authorized by the UN for genocide but not for vague claims that a threat to the peace exists, some additional support might be forthcoming. At the least the *citizens* of small states could support it, because it would help protect them against authoritarian governmental abuse of their human rights. Clarity about the nature of humanitarian intervention also could be crucial at some later point if the UN had to intervene against these citizen's authoritarian government and needed their support.

In sum, the more carefully the concept of humanitarian intervention is understood, the more resistant it will be to abuse and the more politically feasible it will be to employ wisely when needed. For purposes of this analysis, humanitarian intervention means (1) intervening in a country without its consent, (2) using coercive means that often are military but need not be exclusively so, and (3) intending to terminate a government's gross violations of human rights. This definition provides several benefits. The second element, for example, emphasizes the possibility of developing means that are coercive but not highly militarized. The third element clarifies that humanitarian intervention is not collective security action under Chapter VII to counter a threat to the peace. It rejects the tendency among some scholars to use the term "intervention" to refer to all uses of force in international affairs, thereby conflating the use of force in another country's internal affairs, such as in Somalia, and international war, such as Desert Storm to oust Iraq from Kuwait. In addition to the problems mentioned above, such a conflation obscures the particularly problematic uses of military power in trying to shape or even control domestic political life of another country. The first element excludes from "intervention" those UN operations where meaningful consent is given to the UN presence, as in Cambodia, Namibia, and Angola. Where consent is offered, one may understandably have fewer reservations about what the UN should attempt to accomplish. Consent was given at one point by the three relevant governments at war in Croatia and Bosnia, although it may not have been meaningful consent, given the ways in which it was subsequently qualified, withdrawn, or simply ignored. The Bosnian case that Hoffmann deftly examines is not limited to actions for humanitarian intervention, because the war of Serbia against Bosnia can be viewed as a war of external aggression, even though the war of Bosnian Serbs against the Bosnian government can be viewed as a civil war. In either case, international law allows for external parties to give aid to the legitimate government(s) without calling it humanitarian intervention. Relatively clear-cut examples of humanitarian intervention include UN operations in Somalia to provide security for administering food aid, the intervention in Haiti to restore democratic government, and multilateral efforts following Desert Storm to protect Kurds against violence from the Iraqi government.

Even a strict and clear definition of humanitarian intervention, of course, will not cause conditions on the ground to correspond neatly to one's analytic categories. Overlap may occur when a government simultaneously violates human rights at home and commits aggression abroad. UN operations against either would share one difficult condition not associated with traditional peacekeeping: the need to operate without the consent of the target state. The Bosnian case includes violations of norms governing both domestic and inter-state jurisdictions, respectively prohibiting genocide and military aggression. Humanitarian intervention could be justified to counter the former and collective security measures could be authorized to resist the latter. The severe difficulties in the Bosnian case arose not because of any failure to find a legitimate authorization for intervention, but because member governments lacked the willingness to provide human and material resources needed to mitigate the conflict and bring order to the region. The international community demonstrated similar unwillingness in Somalia, Rwanda, Georgia, the Sudan, and elsewhere at the same time. Governments have many short-term self-interested reasons, some deeply entrenched, for refusing to support both humanitarian intervention and collective security actions. The international community needs, on the one hand, to generate increased political support for legitimate humanitarian interventions while, on the other, to close the door to abusive intervention that causes more international disorder or more local suffering. Because the difficulties of this task and governmental resistance to interventions are unlikely to be overcome for a long time, it behooves us to nurture all possible means that might increase compliance with international norms of peace and human rights without relying heavily on problematic uses of military force. The following eight guidelines highlight the search for a third path between doing nothing and sending troops. They harmonize with Hoffmann's goal of maximizing compliance with international norms at minimum cost in human lives, while offering a different emphasis. The proposed path certainly is no panacea. In some instances, states may still choose to do nothing or to deploy troops. Giving attention to a third path is simply intended to provide additional creative space so that governments may feel less need to resign themselves reluctantly to one of only two other possibilities.

2. Guidelines for Intervention

In this historical era, states derive legitimacy,[9] in part, from their citizens. As a result, if a state denies many of its citizens their fundamental rights, the traditional constraint against external intervention in the domestic jurisdiction of a state's sovereignty no longer applies with its previous strength. Hoffmann's position fits well with that of an increasing number of scholars and governments who have recognized "that there is a right to international intervention for humanitarian purposes."[10] Many commentators would argue that the protection of fundamental human rights has now risen to the level of *jus cogens* and that states are bound to uphold these rights.[11] As a former UN representative in Somalia, Mohamed Sahnoun, has said, "Governments cannot invoke sovereignty to prevent humanitarian access to the population. . . . If there is a humanitarian catastrophe, the international community is morally bound to intervene."[12] Although controversy abounds about the content of "fundamental rights" that would trigger intervention, genocide illustrates a gross violation of fundamental rights and serves as a useful point of departure. It is so clearly prohibited by treaty and custom that the international community can be expected to justify intervention against it.

Nonetheless, because the prohibition against external intervention is an important instrument for avoiding conflicts and respecting self-determination, Hoffmann correctly emphasizes that it should not be lightly cast aside. Therefore, the burden of proof should still remain on those who would justify intervention. The following guidelines can inform legitimate justification for humanitarian intervention along a third path and maximize its long-term deterring impact on those who might commit future misdeeds.

First, *to minimize the need to employ military force, the international community should devote far more resources and attention to strategies of conflict mitigation and peace-building.* Well-designed comprehensive efforts can cultivate a culture of compliance and enforcement that will increase respect for a minimal number of fundamental norms. Indeed many of the most horrendous instances of genocide could be prevented if states genuinely wanted to do so. In Rwanda, for example, earlier and more generous use of effective international means to encourage forms of economic and social development that would lead to social integration and relieve population pressure (preventive development), education and training against bigotry (preventive education), international programs of police training and monitoring of domestic law enforcement officials (preventive enforcement), and more forceful efforts to investigate and prosecute earlier crimes against humanity (preventive adjudication) could have made a profound difference in discouraging genocide in 1994. The positive incentives provided by preventive development,[13] which use economic benefits to eliminate conditions that give rise to violence, and other measures designed for long-range peace-building, are vastly underutilized. Negative incentives such as economic sanctions and indictment of those accused of crimes against humanity, which are somewhat coercive yet have the advantage of not being military combat, are also underdeveloped and not used effectively. Though costly, they are less costly and risky than combat, and thereby more likely to win essential international support.

Moreover, comprehensive preventive efforts, utilizing a shrewd

combination of positive and negative incentives, can do much more
than has been done in the past to gain consent for a UN presence.
These efforts could induce a target government to consent to a UN
presence in time of crisis, in which case a serious problem might
be addressed without the need for formal intervention. That result
would make a UN operation legally less controversial, morally more
desirable, and politically more effective. The need to employ military
instruments for humanitarian intervention is almost always a sign
of international failure to deal with fundamental causes of poverty,
prejudice, and inequity. Military means would normally be unnecessary if other instruments were fully utilized in timely fashion.

To mobilize international support for the preceding measures, as
well as to respond to short-term needs for preventive diplomacy and
preventive deployments of peacekeepers, UN officials need to make
the case in detail that using military combat, even under UN auspices, as a means for humanitarian intervention not only would
often be unnecessary if preventive measures were more robust, but
also is frequently unworkable. Military combat as an instrument of
humanitarian intervention usually has low utility for nation-build-
ing or weaving a new social fabric conducive to stability and democracy, as UN operations in Somalia underscored. When asked "Can
you point to a case where [UN] military intervention was used in
a way that turned out to be measured and constructive and didn't
get off track, as seems to have happened in Somalia, or has been
used very ineffectively, as in Bosnia?" Sahnoun responded "I can't."
Even in Cambodia, UN success was based on diplomatic moves
made in advance of UN peacekeeping.[14] In addition, countries
simply are not willing to pay much in terms of money and lives for
carrying out a difficult war for humanitarian purposes, as Europe
and the United States clearly demonstrated in Bosnia, Rwanda, Somalia, and elsewhere in the early 1990s.

Most governments not only have employed spineless diplomacy
in pushing the UN halfheartedly into the former Yugoslavia, as
Hoffmann indicates, they also have used the UN to cover up their
own failures. Governments mandated an ineffective UN presence to
enable them to pretend they were taking action when in reality they
were doing nothing. In such cases, a primary focus on the military

aspects of humanitarian intervention can actually divert attention from effectively employing less militarized elements, such as non-recognition of borders changed through military action, economic sanctions, and war crimes indictments. Such a focus also diverts attention, over the longer run, from pre-conflict peace-building activities that could have been employed to avert the particular crisis at hand, as well as from contemporaneous peace-building that is needed elsewhere to avert future crises.

Second, *the norms intended to trigger humanitarian intervention should be clear, widely accepted, relatively uncontroversial, and specified in advance.* The rights to be upheld must not be derived from a single national or cultural tradition or any particular political or economic ideology.[15] Unacceptable behavior triggering humanitarian intervention would presumably include genocide, systematic denial of food, and interference with humanitarian assistance. But humanitarian intervention to guarantee political freedoms would not receive sufficiently widespread support to warrant intervention for that reason at this historical stage, unless their denial is due to an overtly racist system, as in the case of apartheid. In addition, willingness to restore a democratic government that had been removed through irregular procedures may be an emerging justification for intervention, as the Haitian case demonstrates.[16]

The justification for humanitarian intervention to help restore a democratically selected government that has been ousted by a coup or violent means is made easier because the local people presumably would agree with the UN purpose and welcome peacekeepers. After overcoming the initial opposition of the usurping regime, UN forces could operate more in a police mode than a military mode. Sovereignty would not be directly violated because it would have been previously compromised by the usurping officials; in a sense, the people have given "anticipatory consent" to the UN operation by their earlier democratic process of electing the ousted government. After the rightful government is restored to power it presumably would give official consent to the UN presence.

To clarify conditions that might trigger intervention, governments should implement Hoffmann's positive suggestion to negotiate one or more treaties that would specify the circumstances in which collective humanitarian intervention could be authorized. Such treaties could establish a firm, clear, legal framework for identifying the forms of intervention that are allowed, the conditions warranting intervention, and the authorities entitled to intervene. The international community should also consider seriously Hoffmann's recommendation that governments establish as a condition for recognition of new states the right of the international community to intervene to assure that the country complies with specified criteria, including respect for minority rights and democracy.[17]

Third, *any violations that may prompt intervention should be clear and well documented.* For this purpose there is no substitute for UN observers on the scene to report honestly what they see. The tendency of some personnel in the United Nations Protection Force (UNPROFOR) in Bosnia to gloss over, understate, and actually mislead others about crimes against humanity is totally unacceptable and almost certain, if repeated, to doom UN efforts to failure in the long run. UN monitoring capacities in general need to be upgraded. Moreover, specific UN data-gathering capacities for investigating and prosecuting war crimes and crimes against humanity need to be systematized, sophisticated, and greatly enlarged. In addition to UN observers, the Organization for Security and Cooperation in Europe has deployed nine long-term missions, further illustrating the forms of external observation that can help mitigate violent conflict.

Fourth, *any intervening agency should have widespread legitimacy and possess a limited but real autonomy from separate states in decision-making and action.* In most cases, Security Council decisions and operations carried out under UN auspices provide the most legitimacy. Tom Weiss is probably correct that "UN decision-making is the only available and sensible way to coordinate global responses to genocidal misery and massive human rights abuse in war zones around the world."[18] Hoffmann indicates that regional organizations such as the Organization of American States or the Organization of African Unity may conduct a legitimate intervention, but they should of course operate within Charter guidelines and keep the UN informed of their actions.

Nothing is more important for UN operations than their legitimacy. When it is high, missions are far more likely to succeed. On the other hand, "no amount of political will or military firepower can compensate for the failure to establish legitimacy."[19] Because existing Security Council membership and procedures reflect the diplomatic world of 1945, structural reforms to limit the use of the veto for permanent members and to increase representativeness, consultation, and the transparency of Council deliberations could enhance the legitimacy of Council actions.[20]

To maintain high legitimacy, intervention should not be allowed to serve particular national agendas or narrowly self-serving goals of the permanent members collectively. Decisions should emphasize equity and reciprocity whenever multilateral interventions are undertaken because these enhance the expectation of legitimate behavior and nurture an international culture of compliance, making the use of military force less likely over the long run. To discourage narrowly self-serving interventions and possibly escalating counterinterventions, it seems to me wise to reject Hoffmann's suggestion that would allow unilateral military intervention when the UN is unable to act.[21]

Despite this allowance for unilateral action, Hoffmann acknowledges that if his proposed criteria for intervention had been adopted and fully honored, U.S. interventions in Guatemala, Grenada, Panama, El Salvador, and Nicaragua would all have been illegitimate.[22] If so, why encourage the possibility that similar interventions might occur in the future by allowing unilateral interventions at all? The willingness of great powers to take illegitimate advantage of interventionary loopholes, even by states strongly affirming human rights, confirms the need to close loopholes and to make the Security Council as democratic as possible (to limit abuses stemming from lack of representation). To discourage great powers from violating the principles of equity and reciprocity when their own issues come before the Council, the international community also should gradually qualify and eventually phase out the veto power.

Hoffmann correctly acknowledges that there can be no UN military enforcement against those governments possessing "a major modern army."[23] But he offers no correctives. Yet such a flatly inequitable condition, if left totally unaddressed while humanitarian concerns are raised with increasing frequency, would constantly call into question the legitimacy of UN interventions. One modest antidote to inequity, of course, would be to ensure that the authoritative decision-makers in the Security Council are more representative of all the world's peoples. But that is insufficient. Significantly, the inequity posed by nonenforcement against military powers will be most glaring and destabilizing if the chosen instrumentality for enforcement is mainly military. Against modest UN military power, larger national military powers will not be moved. In contrast, if nonmilitary instruments were strengthened, they could apply also to the militarily powerful. The reason for the failure of the powerful states to strengthen these legal instruments, a skeptic might think, is because they could apply more equitably to the powerful than could the military instrument. Equally unsettling, the existing inequities in enforcement, which in practice shield military powers from intervention, provide incentives for would-be law-breakers throughout the world to acquire more military power so they too will not need to respect international humanitarian norms or face possible UN intervention.

In underemphasizing nonmilitary instruments, observers also underrepresent the interests of the weak and too easily ignore the importance of reciprocity in strengthening the international normative structure. To be sure, if one thinks only in military terms, "the UN lacks the possibility even to conceive of a coercive intervention in the domestic affairs of a major power. . . . "[24] Yet it is not unthinkable that leaders of major powers could be subject to similar investigatory and indictment procedures for crimes against humanity that have been used against officials in the former Yugoslavia and Rwanda, building on postwar precedents for defeated officials after World War II. It is not unimaginable that economic sanctions or citizen boycotts could some day discourage Chinese human rights violations in Tibet. Financial penalties can be levied against government officials and private citizens in major powers. Indeed, the latter happens now for a variety of reasons. Sometimes international monetary decisions *do* constitute a form of "coercive intervention in the domestic affairs of a major power" even though they are not military. Failure to emphasize such possibilities acquiesces in unnecessary enforcement inequities and impedes the development of more robust international legal processes.

To succeed, leaders of UN operations need to maintain legitimacy not only in the capitals of the world but also in the eyes of the local populations where they operate. The largest risk for a UN humanitarian intervention, John Steinbrunner has concluded, is that UN personnel may become "the organizing force of resistance" and thereby engage in self-defeating behavior.[25] UN peacekeepers will face an uphill battle for legitimacy when intervening in small poor countries in the future if the foregoing measures are not implemented to redress existing inequities and privileges for the rich and powerful.

Because member governments may be reluctant to offer financial and personnel support when humanitarian intervention is needed, providing the UN with more autonomy to act would also increase its effectiveness. Present troublesome constraints include the indifference of member governments to taking collective action, their resistance to contributing necessary resources, their hesitation about preventive deployment of UN forces, the UN's incapacity for rapid deployment of forces, the lack of staying power once an operation is underway, and poor training, discipline, and coordination of some ad hoc forces.

If the UN established its own permanent constabulary force, recruited from among individuals who may volunteer from all countries of the world, it could deploy a well-trained, reliable force, willing to take action even though risks and costs might deter member governments from contributing their own forces or placing them under UN command.[26] Moreover, with an immediately available, special purpose force, the UN could maximize the prospects for intervening more in a constabulary role than a military one.[27] Such a force would be less subject to the charges of national partisanship that attend the contingents of national armed forces making up existing ad hoc UN forces. A permanent volunteer force would give the UN a desirable degree of autonomy and the ability to intervene at the time and in the form that would minimize violence. To succeed, of course, the UN would need independent means of raising revenue to provide for such a force.[28]

To take a second example of the need for additional UN autonomy, the UN could benefit enormously from establishing worldwide, independent broadcast facilities to provide an independent source of information about issues of violent conflict, guide people to reliable safe areas in times of crisis, and counter sources of information that cynical political leaders often use to fan the flames of hostility and bigotry. In Rwanda "a single radio station urging total genocide is believed to have had a major impact on the population. Conversely, a radio station in Cambodia that preached a message of reconciliation is credited by U.N. observers with a significant positive impact. In the Rwanda case, substitution of a different message . . . would have had obvious advantages. . . ."[29] If comprehensive efforts, similar to these illustrations, would be studied, widely discussed, and implemented, we would not be limited to "a world in which cosmopolitanism remains largely the faith of (some) intellectuals and of international civil servants. . . . "[30] Cynical leaders would have a harder time whipping up genocidal violence against minorities, and perpetrators would have ample warning that the international community would make serious efforts to prosecute them.

Fifth, *the nature of the means employed in international intervention should be carefully constrained by internationally established norms against excessive use of force and the protection of innocent people.* This is essential for maintaining high legitimacy for UN operations. Because humanitarian intervention poses enormous difficulties in execution on the ground, it preferably should be carried out by a permanent UN constabulary force such as proposed above, specially trained and equipped, and directly under the control of the UN. Until such a force is created, it might be wise to discourage the use of military means in humanitarian intervention. Many governments are most reluctant to place their personnel under UN command in risky contexts, precisely the time when impartiality is most needed. Because the times when the United States and other great powers will cede command to the UN are the times when the mission is least dangerous, operations will be least genuinely *international* in character when enforcement is most highly militarized.

Sixth, *the goals of intervention should be (1) to stop wrongdoing by those engaging in misconduct rather than to attack an entire nation, (2) to protect victims, and (3) to strengthen precedents, institutions, and an international culture of compliance that will increasingly deter future misdeeds.* Economic sanctions can be an important coercive instrument for encouraging a culture of compliance with fundamental humanitarian norms, although they certainly provide no panacea; they are slow and may inflict hardship on innocent people. UN economic sanctions against Serbia nudged President Slobodan Milosevic toward a peaceful settlement in 1995, even at some expense to the Bosnian Serbs.[31] Although the arms embargo on the Serbian and Bosnian governments handicapped the Bosnians and aided the Serbs, who had inherited Yugoslav weapons, the sanctions, despite their porousness, did punish Serbia economically and helped bring Milosevic to the negotiating table. Of course economic sanctions should also be governed by the principle of minimizing negative effects to ensure they do not themselves violate fundamental human rights. They should be used with a combination of restraint and determination. Hoffmann gives little attention to imagining how either positive economic incentives or negative economic sanctions might contribute to a culture of compliance. The UN could no doubt develop better ways of focusing sanctions on elites responsible for misconduct, to avoid some of the negative humanitarian consequences from the use of sanctions in the past. Sanctions should often be imposed earlier in a rising crisis, to give them time to work. They should never cover food, medical supplies, or needs for fundamental life support of the population of a country. Instead, they could be used to deprive elites of economic gain, international travel and communication, and access to any assets they may possess outside a country shielding their activity. If governing elites interfered with food aid going to their subjects, this would constitute an additional reason for intervention and possibly for changing the government in question.

To discourage some human rights abuses, sanctions need not aim at bringing a society to its knees, as many people commonly assume, but instead at taking away enough economic benefits of the privileged in the target society to encourage them to comply with a few fundamental humanitarian norms. Rather than hope for a quick fix, the UN might develop the ability to sustain sanctions indefinitely, as occurred with some success in changing the behavior of the exponents of apartheid in South Africa. Such sanctions may not save today's victims of injustice, but if everyone throughout the world community knew in advance that elites would be deprived of economic advantages and international interactions if they crossed specified thresholds of misbehavior, this approach would influence much elite behavior in the long run. Although individuals who are pinpointed as wrongdoers could, after due process of investigation and judgment, have their international assets frozen, such measures were not implemented to their utmost even against the Haitian elite that the UN opposed, primarily because European bankers dragged their feet over disclosing ownership of secret accounts. Yet more political support to overcome such resistance can be generated. Intervening governments have no moral entitlement to ask any soldier or civilian policeman to risk his or her life in interventionary actions until these governments insist that their own bankers freeze the assets of those indicted for violating international norms.

A second underdeveloped form of coercion, also not given much weight by Hoffmann, is attempting to hold individuals, rather than entire societies, accountable for behavior violating fundamental norms, such as genocide. One profoundly important merit of prosecuting war crimes and crimes against humanity is that legal processes enable the international community to take action against individuals committing misdeeds rather than against an entire nation. Even if such action is not fully successful because many accused may, at least for a time, be shielded by a crime-approving government, it offers some advantages over (1) military combat, which kills the innocent as often as the guilty, and (2) economic sanctions, which penalize only imprecisely. Through the legal process, through indictments of persons who have committed misdeeds, regardless of nationality, the UN can demonstrate that it is not anti-Serbian or anti-Hutu but is anti-genocide. The only workable solution to the problem of effective UN enforcement in the long run is to focus less on attempting, with enormous difficulties, to enforce norms militarily and collectively on an entire society, and instead to enforce law on individuals who are responsible for illegal conduct. In the long run, incentives and sanctions must focus on deterring the actual wrongdoers.

The international community is failing to utilize the important Nuremberg precedent that, when international rules protecting fundamental human rights conflict with state laws or military practice, an individual must disobey the state laws and practice to honor the international norms. Hoffmann dismisses war crimes tribunals, first of all, because they cannot apprehend many wrongdoers. To be sure, that is a serious problem, but at least in some cases people can be arrested and tried.[32] In addition, because there is no statute of limitations for such crimes, any person indicted but unwilling to face trial is in practice barred from international travel forever. Using its existing powers, the Security Council could and should impose sanctions against any society refusing to extradite indicted persons for trial by a duly authorized international tribunal. Since governments change over time, no person committing crimes could be assured that he or she would *never* be tried. Even the possibility of someday being held accountable can have a deterring impact.

Theodor Meron has persuasively argued that collecting evidence and preparing indictments could be profoundly influential in the long run even if leaders cannot be tried in the short run.[33] More knowledge of and emphasis on the crime of genocide would have a deterring effect on political leaders and on soldiers or citizens who otherwise might commit atrocities. If indicted individuals refusing to face trial would lose international economic resources and the right to travel and communicate outside the territory of those who would shield them, and if penalties were also brought against those shielding the indicted, such policies could have an important deterring effect in the long run.

The international community, through the UN Security Council, should also specify that any person who impedes authorized UN enforcement personnel is indictable for crimes against the peace. It is outrageous that Serbian officials in Bosnia have been quoted by name in the newspapers after capturing UN peacekeepers and holding them hostage, claiming the right to attack UN personnel unless the UN meets certain of their war demands.[34]

A second reason often given for not focusing on war crimes investigations is that, in addition to not making a significant positive difference, they may even have a negative impact. For example, efforts to prosecute war crimes may alienate those leaders, possibly under investigation, whose cooperation is needed to arrange a cease-fire. This is a serious problem in the former Yugoslavia, yet to downplay the importance of prosecuting war crimes in favor of emphasizing external military intervention or to make normative compromises for the sake of negotiating progress may also fail to achieve a desirable outcome. As Hoffmann's analysis makes clear, conventional diplomatic and military efforts by Europeans failed to produce positive results and probably prevented more clearheaded initiatives from the beginning. Each round of negotiations for a cease-fire ended by ratifying new gains made on the ground by military aggressors. The UN arms embargo aided the aggressor. European diplomacy acquiesced in ethnic cleansing. Would the results have been worse if, at the outset, the international community simply refused to recognize breakaway states without reliable international guarantees for minorities, refused to accept any change of borders through the use of force, refused to legitimize ethnic cleansing and military aggression through negotiated redrawing of the map, attempted to reinforce the standard of nonaggression and respect for human rights through more focused economic sanctions and positive economic incentives for normatively desirable behavior, provided humanitarian assistance, and investigated and prosecuted crimes against humanity more intensively? If this approach had been followed and war broke out nonetheless, many of those accused of crimes admittedly could not have been arrested promptly and tried. But because they could be subject to arrest indefinitely into the future and forced to stay within the territories of those who would for an uncertain length of time shield them from the law, perhaps at some penalty and ignominy to the latter, it would have served as a sterner warning for others in the future. With such an approach, at the least, the rules against aggression and genocide would have been reaffirmed more firmly and the misconduct of individuals could have become a central focus of the media. Compared to ineffective UN military intervention, the costs of prosecuting war crimes are not high. The main price that governments have not been willing to pay is to overcome their reluctance to see people of all nationalities, including their own, be subject to the law.

To reinforce the deterring strength of international tribunals, it seems extremely important to adhere to Ambassador Madeleine Albright's commitment not to compromise war crimes indictments: There "should be no question that political and military leaders may be held criminally accountable if they do not stop atrocities by their followers or do not punish those responsible."[35] U.S. officials have repeatedly indicated that indictments should not be erased in order to achieve a peace agreement; they have "publicly and emphatically insisted . . . that there will be no amnesty for those charged with war crimes in Bosnia."[36] To bolster the deterring impact of war crimes investigations and indictments, the United Nations should strengthen its data-gathering capacities. Member governments should be encouraged to provide evidence for UN tribunals from their national information services. Yet because some governments will withhold information for political reasons, the UN and a permanent international criminal court, if one is established, should maintain an independent, expert capacity for systematic collection of evidence on war crimes.

Finally, *United Nations officials and national leaders should focus on the need for a broad, comprehensive approach to counter gross violations of human rights, emphasizing the growth of an ethos or culture of compliance and of nonmilitary yet coercive enforcement.* Such an approach would enable the UN to focus upon what it does best: clarify norms, legitimize international monitoring and nonmilitary enforcement of them, and delegitimize unilateral actions in violation of fundamental norms of peace and human rights.[37] Although no single initiative by itself can make a sufficient difference, by encouraging political leaders at many levels and in all regions of the world to draw upon normative strengths in religious traditions, secular world views, education, journalism, and economic, political, and social institutions, a culture of compliance and enforcement can take root and flourish.

Critics of the approach proposed here argue that the international community cannot be coercive without using military instruments. Yet economic sanctions, fines, war crimes indictments, and police enforcement illustrate (and certainly do not exhaust) the possibilities for being coercive without engaging in combat. By themselves these instruments cannot promise effectiveness in every case. But then neither can military power always ensure success in accomplishing one's mission, as U.S. and Soviet exponents of their respective military missions in Vietnam and Afghanistan can confirm. States should expand their collective nonmilitary instruments for upholding humanitarian norms because such instruments hold some promise, compared to military means, not because they promise a panacea. In any case, no one can force states to rely exclusively on nonmilitary means, so military instruments will still be available, even if a third path is pursued. Because military options would not be eliminated, those comfortable in relying on them need not reject developing a third path in addition to the options of either not intervening or intervening with military forces.

Critics also argue that employing nonmilitary means may increase tensions and cause a target state to respond militarily. Such an outcome is of course possible, but not inevitable. If the risks are too large to accept, then all forms of intervention may be dubious. In any case, the more effective the nonmilitary means become, the less pressure there will be for at least one actor to escalate the conflict to military combat, thus giving a better prospect of avoiding combat than would exist without strengthened nonmilitary instruments.

The preceding seven guidelines attempt to take counterarguments seriously. They emanate from much of the cautionary advice that Stanley Hoffmann has laid out so well. At the same time, they encourage a different diplomatic emphasis, admittedly requiring widespread education and new transnational political action to implement. They also grow from a deep skepticism about the utility and feasibility of opening the door more widely to military combat, as opposed to police enforcement, in the service of humanitarian intervention. More insight, energy, and resources devoted to improving preventive measures and nonmilitary coercive instruments to deter gross violations of human rights could yield rewarding dividends in the long run.

NOTES

1. Lincoln Bloomfield, for example, has concluded that "The emerging collective security system should . . . look more like law enforcement than war-fighting. Credible and politically acceptable collective security scenarios will thus initially feature not armies, navies, and air forces but a step-by-step police process that mimics familiar domestic law enforcement. . . . " He recommends national earmarking, "not of vast armies but of trained technicians and US marshal-type 'peace officers.' " Lincoln P. Bloomfield, "Collective Security and US Interests," in *Collective Security in a Changing World*, ed. Thomas G. Weiss (Boulder, Colo.: Lynne Rienner, 1993), 201.

2. Hoffmann, chapter 2, 23.

3. Ibid.

4. For a penetrating discussion of humanitarian intervention and the theory of collective security, see Raimo Väyrynen, *Enforcement and Humanitarian Intervention: Two Faces of Collective Action by the United Nations*, Occasional Paper 8:OP:2 (University of Notre Dame: Joan B. Kroc Institute, 1995). Väyrynen recommends keeping the enforcement of collective security separate from humanitarian intervention as categories of international action: " . . . despite the practical intertwining of collective enforcement and humanitarian intervention, they should be considered separate legal and political categories" (p. 11).

5. Hoffmann, chapter 3, 54–55.

6. Ibid., 53.

7. For example, the United States provided such a rationale when intervening with U.S. troops in the Dominican Republic in 1965.

8. Hoffmann, chapter 2, 22.

9. A state derives legitimacy through widespread support from its citizens and by acting in conformity with law and established traditions. International legitimacy derives from acting in conformity with existing legal and customary norms, honoring procedures outlined in the UN Charter for authoritative decisions on intervention, and having political approval from many nations and cultural regions. As the authors of a well-known

text put it, "the UN Charter is the closest thing that we have to a global constitution. When state actors comply with the Charter and use UN procedures, their policies acquire the legitimacy that stems from international law. They also acquire the legitimacy that stems from collective political approval, the realization of which is one of the more important tasks performed by the UN." See Thomas G. Weiss, David P. Forsythe, and Roger A. Coate, *The United Nations and Changing World Politics* (Boulder, Colo.: Westview, 1994), 10.

10. Thomas G. Weiss, "Triage: Humanitarian Interventions in a New Era," *World Policy Journal* 11 (Spring 1994): 59; Massoud Barzani, "Hope Restored: Benefits of Humanitarian Intervention," *Harvard International Review* 16 (Fall 1993), 18–19.

11. Fernando R. Teson, *Humanitarian Intervention: An Inquiry Into Law and Morality* (Dobbs Ferry, N.Y.: Transnational Publishers, 1988).

12. Mohamed Sahnoun, "An Interview with Mohamed Sahnoun," *Middle East Report* 24, no. 2–3 (1994): 29.

13. Positive incentives include investing shared financial resources explicitly to promote social integration and discourage mutually reinforcing social cleavages and single-identity conflicts. The United Nations Development Program has described measures of both "preventive and curative development [that] are needed to support processes of social integration." The UN operations in Somalia during 1993 alone, for example, cost more than $2 billion. Wise investment of a similar amount in socio-economic development a decade earlier could have averted the crisis altogether. Preventive development emphasizes programs aimed at creating the opportunity for everyone, regardless of class or ethnic group, to develop her or his own capacities; encouraging broadly based economic activity so that everyone has equal access to economic opportunities; designing affirmative action programs that help weaker groups to gain proportionally more than others.

14. As Sahnoun has reported, "it's really difficult to point to a situation where an armed intervention represented a solution. The solution most of the time was found diplomatically, and the armed intervention came either as enforcement or as a peacekeeping operation for a solution which had been found before. This was the case in Mozambique as well as in Cambodia." See Sahnoun, "An Interview," 30.

15. See John Steinbrunner, "Memorandum: Civil Violence as an International Security Problem," in *Protecting the Dispossessed: A Challenge to the International Community,* ed. Francis M. Deng (Washington, D.C.: Brookings Institution, 1993), 156–57.

16. Lori Fisler Damrosch, "Introduction," in *Enforcing Restraint: Col-*

lective Intervention in Internal Conflicts, ed. Damrosch (New York: Council
on Foreign Relations, 1993), 12–13.

17. Hoffmann, chapter 2, 25.

18. Weiss, "Triage," 66.

19. Steinbrunner, "Memorandum," 156–57.

20. Lori Fisler Damrosch, "Concluding Reflections," in *Enforcing Restraint,* 359.

21. Hoffmann, chapter 2, 22.

22. Ibid., 23.

23. Ibid., 27.

24. Hoffmann, chapter 2, 33.

25. Steinbrunner, "Memorandum," 156–57.

26. See the Netherlands proposal for a full-time, professional, permanently available UN Legion. Hans Van Mierlo, *Address by Hans Van Mierlo, Minister of Foreign Affairs, 49th Session of the General Assembly, 27 September* (New York: Kingdom of the Netherlands, 1994), 6–7; The Netherlands, "A UN Rapid Deployment Brigade" (April, 1995). Canada has proposed a rapid reaction force, employing a "Vanguard Concept" in which the UN would assemble from member states a multi-functional force of up to 5,000 military and civilian personnel. The UN would give the force specialized training and could rapidly deploy it under the control of a proposed operational-level UN headquarters responsible for planning and advance preparations. Standby forces would be provided by member states, through arrangements made with the Secretariat, offering personnel to participate in peace operations. See Government of Canada, *Towards a Rapid Reaction Capability for the United Nations* (Ottawa: Government of Canada, 1995).

27. To illustrate the damaging delays of ad hoc forces, in April 1992 the Security Council belatedly decided to send peacekeepers to Somalia, but they did not begin to arrive until December of that year. See Adam Roberts, "Humanitarian War: Military Intervention and Human Rights," *International Affairs* 69 (July 1993), 439. Mohamed Sahnoun believes that if the international community had intervened earlier and more effectively, much of the catastrophe that unfolded could have been avoided. Sahnoun, *Somalia: The Missed Opportunities* (Washington, D.C.: United States Institute of Peace Press, 1994).

28. See Robert Johansen, "Reforming the United Nations to Eliminate War," *Transnational Law and Contemporary Problems* 4, no. 2 (Fall 1994): 455–502.

29. Malcolm H. Wiener, *Non-Lethal Technologies: Military Options and Implications* (New York: Council on Foreign Relations, 1995), 7.

30. Hoffmann, chapter 2, 28.

31. For example, Milosevic allowed the Croatians to reconquer territory previously taken and held by the Bosnian Serbs in Krajina. Roger Cohen reported that "the Krajina was sold by President Milosevic as the necessary precursor to a Croatian-Serbian settlement." See "Finally Torn Apart, The Balkans Can Hope," *The New York Times,* 3 September 1995, E6.

32. In Rwanda, for example, many of the accused are not being shielded by any government.

33. Theodor Meron, "The Case for War Crimes Trials in Yugoslavia," *Foreign Affairs* 72 (Summer 1993): 122–35.

34. See Roger Cohen, "Bosnian Serbs Call for Talks; U.N. Refuses, Seeing a Ploy," *New York Times,* 1 June 1995, A1; Chuck Sudetic, "Bosnian Serbs Set Free 43 U.N. Troops Held Hostage," *New York Times,* 1 December 1994, A10.

35. Madeleine K. Albright, "Bosnia in Light of the Holocaust: War Crimes Tribunals," *U.S. Department of State Dispatch* 5 (April 18, 1994): 210.

36. See Stephen Engelberg, "Tribunal Asks U.S. for Pledge on War Crimes," *New York Times,* 3 November 1995, A5.

37. On the utility of the UN's ability to nurture normative development, see Michael N. Barnett, "The United Nations and Global Security: The Norm is Mightier Than the Sword," *Ethics and International Affairs* 9 (1995): 37–54.

5

HOFFMANN'S KANTIAN JUSTIFICATION FOR HUMANITARIAN INTERVENTION
James P. Sterba

THOSE WHO undertake the task of commentator are usually concerned to find fault with the work under discussion, and the quality of their comments is usually measured by the significance of the faults they uncover. Or more precisely, since the reality and significance of a work's faults are usually contested, at least by the author, the success of a commentator is usually measured by the intensity or liveliness of the exchange that the commentator manages to provoke. Commenting in this way is, of course, akin to fighting a battle or making war. Arguments are attacked, shot down (like a plane) or sunk (like a ship). Theses are defended or demolished (like the walls of a city). Ideas (like people) are killed or destroyed. But why should war-making be our model for being a commentator? I think that we need a more peaceful and cooperative model. So I want to try something different. What I propose to do is, first, show how Stanley Hoffmann's norms for humanitarian intervention can be seen to follow from a particular moral approach to practical problems, second, discuss briefly his specific recommendations for the Yugoslavian situation, and third, show how, by making a slight change, his account can gain a rhetorical advantage.

To begin, I want to distinguish a moral approach to practical problems from various nonmoral approaches. Nonmoral approaches to practical problems include the *legal approach* (what the law requires with respect to particular practical problems), the *special interest approach* (what the special interests of the parties require with respect to particular practical problems), and the *scientific approach* (how practical problems can best be accounted for or understood). To call these approaches nonmoral, of course, does not imply that they are immoral. All that is implied is that the requirements of these approaches may or may not accord with the requirements of morality.

What, then, essentially characterizes a moral approach to practical problems? I suggest that there are two essential features to such an approach:

1. The approach is prescriptive, that is, it issues in prescriptions, such as "do this" and "don't do that."
2. The approach's prescriptions are acceptable to every party affected by them.

The first feature distinguishes a moral approach from a scientific approach because a scientific approach is not prescriptive. The second feature distinguishes a moral approach from both a legal approach and a special interest approach because the prescriptions that accord best with the law or serve the special interest of particular parties may not be acceptable to every party affected by them.

Here the notion of "acceptable" means "ought to be accepted" or "is reasonable to accept" and not simply "is capable of being accepted." Understood in this way, certain prescriptions may be acceptable even though they are not actually accepted by every party affected by them. For example, a particular welfare program may be acceptable even though many people oppose it because it involves an increased tax burden. Likewise, certain prescriptions may be unacceptable even though they have been accepted by everyone affected by them. For example, it may be that most women have been socialized to accept prescriptions requiring them to fill certain social roles even though these prescriptions are unacceptable because they impose second-class status on women.

1. Alternative Moral Approaches to Practical Problems

Using the two essential features of a moral approach to practical problems, let us consider three principal alternative moral approaches to practical problems: a *Utilitarian Approach,* an *Aristotelian Approach,* and a *Kantian Approach.* The basic principle of a Utilitarian Approach is:

> Do those actions that maximize the net utility or satisfaction of every party affected by them.

A Utilitarian Approach qualifies as a moral approach because it is prescriptive and because it can be argued that its prescriptions are acceptable to every party affected by them since they take the utility or satisfaction of all those parties equally into account.

But are such calculations of utility possible? Admittedly, they are difficult to make. At the same time, such calculations seem to serve as a basis for many public discussions. Once President Reagan, addressing a group of black business leaders, asked whether blacks were better off because of the Great Society programs, and although many disagreed with the answer he gave, no one found his question unanswerable. Thus faced with the exigencies of measuring utility, a Utilitarian Approach simply counsels that we do our best to determine what maximizes net utility and act on the result.

The second approach to be considered is an Aristotelian Approach. Its basic principle is:

> Do those actions that would further the proper development of every affected party.

This approach also qualifies as a moral approach because it is prescriptive and because it can be argued that its prescriptions are acceptable to every party affected by them.

There are, however, different versions of this approach. According to some versions, we can determine through the use of reason what constitutes proper development. Other versions disagree. For example, many religious traditions rely on revelation to determine proper development. However, although an Aristotelian Approach can take these various forms, I want to focus on what is probably its philosophically most interesting form. That form specifies proper development in terms of virtuous activity and understands virtuous activity to preclude intentionally doing evil that good may come of it. In this form, an Aristotelian Approach conflicts most radically

with a Utilitarian Approach, which requires intentionally doing evil
whenever a *greater* good would come of it.

The third approach to be considered is a Kantian Approach. This
approach has its origins in seventeenth- and eighteenth-century social contract theories, which tended to rely on actual contracts to
specify moral requirements. However, actual contracts may or may
not have been made, and, even if they were made, they may or may
not have been moral or fair. This led Immanuel Kant and contemporary Kantian John Rawls to resort to hypothetical contracts to
ground moral requirements. A difficulty with this approach is in
determining under what conditions a hypothetical contract is fair
and moral. Currently, the most favored Kantian Approach is specified by the following basic principle:

> Do those actions that parties behind an imaginary veil
> of ignorance would unanimously agree should be done.

This imaginary veil extends to most particular facts about each
party—anything that would bias a party's choice or stand in the
way of a unanimous agreement. Accordingly, the imaginary veil of
ignorance would mask the knowledge parties have of their abilities
and resources, but not their knowledge of such general information
as would be contained in political, social, economic, and psychological theories. A Kantian Approach qualifies as a moral approach
because it is prescriptive and because it can be argued that its prescriptions would be acceptable to every party affected by them since
they would be agreed to by every party affected behind an imaginary
veil of ignorance.

2. Assessing Alternative Moral Approaches

Needless to say, each of these moral approaches has its strengths
and weaknesses. The main strength of a Utilitarian Approach is that
once the relevant utilities are determined, there is an effective decision-making procedure that can be used to resolve practical problems. After determining the relevant utilities, all that remains is to
total the net utilities and choose the alternative with the highest net
utility. The basic weakness of this approach, however, is that it does

not give sufficient weight to the distribution of utility among the relevant parties. All that matters for this approach is maximizing total utility, and the distribution of utility among the affected parties is taken into account only insofar as it contributes toward the attainment of that goal.

By contrast, the main strength of an Aristotelian Approach in the form we are considering is that it limits the means that can be chosen in pursuit of good consequences. In particular, it absolutely prohibits intentionally doing evil that good may come of it. However, although some limit on the means available for the pursuit of good consequences seems desirable, the main weakness of this version of an Aristotelian Approach is that the limit it imposes is too strong. Indeed, exceptions to this limit would seem to be justified whenever the evil to be done is:

1. Trivial (e.g., stepping on someone's foot to get out of a crowded subway).
2. Easily reparable (e.g., lying to a temporarily depressed friend to keep her from committing suicide).
3. Sufficiently outweighed by the consequences of the action (e.g., shooting one of 200 civilian hostages to prevent in the only way possible the execution of all 200).

Still another weakness of this approach is that it lacks an effective decision-making procedure for resolving practical problems. Beyond imposing limits on the means that can be employed in the pursuit of good consequences, the advocates of this approach have not agreed on criteria for selecting among the available alternatives.

A strength of a Kantian Approach is that, like an Aristotelian Approach, it seeks to limit the means available for the pursuit of good consequences. However, unlike the version of the Aristotelian Approach we considered, a Kantian Approach does not impose an absolute limit on intentionally doing evil that good may come of it. Behind the veil of ignorance, parties would surely agree that if the evil were either trivial, easily reparable, or sufficiently outweighed by the consequences, there would be an adequate justification for permitting it. Another strength of the Kantian Approach is that, like the Utilitarian Approach, it provides an effective decision-making procedure for resolving practical problems. By thus combining strengths of both the Aristotelian and Utilitarian Approaches without their weaknesses, the Kantian Approach can be seen to be morally preferable to these two other approaches to practical problems.

3. Application to Hoffmann's Account

I now want to suggest that what I take to be Stanley Hoffmann's basic norm for humanitarian intervention can be derived from the Kantian Approach to moral problems. One formulation that Hoffmann gives this basic norm of humanitarian intervention is the following:

> Sovereignty can be overridden whenever the behavior of the state, even within its own territory, threatens the existence of elementary human rights abroad, and whenever the protection of the rights of its own members can be assured only from the outside.

It seems clear that parties behind a veil of ignorance, choosing in imagined ignorance of their own capabilities and resources, would favor just such a norm to protect their fundamental interests. Moreover, I think this norm would be chosen irrespective of whether we were to interpret the parties to the agreement to be human individuals or nation-states, as long as nation-states are understood to simply represent the collective interests of their members. This is because whether as human individuals or as nation-states that represent the collective interests of their members, the parties would want their fundamental interests protected, and since they are choosing in imagined ignorance of their own capabilities and resources for protecting those interests, they would favor external intervention to protect those interests when that was required.

4. A Possible Difficulty with Hoffmann's Account

I now want to discuss briefly a possible difficulty with Stanley Hoffmann's specific recommendations for coercive humanitarian intervention. The difficulty is this: the more specific norms that Hoffmann set out in his first lecture (chapter 2) may conflict with the even more specific moral judgments about the Yugoslavian situation that he made in his second lecture (chapter 3) and elsewhere.[1] Hoffmann judges the lack of coercive intervention against the Serbs to be "a blot on Western consciences" and "a political and moral mistake." But what kind of a moral mistake is it? Is it a mistake of individual states or a mistake of the UN or of regional organizations? Hoffmann seems to suggest that the mistake is primarily a mistake of the UN or of regional organizations, that they either should have intervened collectively or should have sanctioned unilateral intervention. But he also, I think, suggests, or at least I would want to suggest, that even in the absence of UN or regional approval, the United States, or France, or both together, should have intervened militarily to try to stop the Serbs from their outrageous human rights violations, preferably early on in the conflict. Hoffmann mentions one moment early in the conflict when a threat of resorting to force might have been highly effective:

> [T]his was at the time of the bombing of Dubrovnik by the Serbs during the war with Croatia in December of 1991; at that moment the commander of NATO in Europe called on the Chairman of the Joint Chiefs of Staff in Washington, General Powell, and suggested that there be a raid against the Serbs because NATO had a fleet and planes were ready. General Powell allegedly said "We do deserts, we don't do mountains."[2]

Hoffmann suggests coercive intervention to try to stop the Serbs' bombing of the city of Dubrovnik would have been justified, and I think that it would have been justified even if it had required unilateral intervention by the United States.

The problem, as I see it, is that such intervention might be ruled out by Hoffmann's more specific norms of humanitarian intervention that he presented in his first lecture if they were not approved by the UN or regional organizations. Now the reason why Hoffmann requires UN or regional approval for unilateral coercive intervention is that he sees a need for "an impartial agency that determines that the cause is good and assures that the intervener has no other motive than the enforcement of what is right."[3] But as Hoffmann himself makes clear in his analysis of the Yugoslavian situation, UN or regional approval was denied in this case for less admirable reasons until quite late in the conflict and not for lack of a good cause or good motives. So I think we can conclude that there is no moral justification for requiring UN or regional approval in this case. This means that the United States and France, for example, should have coercively intervened against the Serbs, even in the absence of UN or regional approval.

It might be objected that in light of the opposition and criticism of the recent NATO bombings of the arms depots and bases of the Bosnian Serbs, comparable unilateral action against Serb aggression by the United States or France earlier in the conflict would surely have drawn even more opposition and criticism.[4] But it is arguable that these NATO bombings have actually helped to bring the Serbs to accept the current cease-fire and timetable for negotiating a peace treaty. Might not earlier unilateral action by the United States or France, particularly during the senseless bombarding of the city of Dubrovnik, have produced a comparable reaction from the Serbs and thus avoided the enormous loss of life and property that has occurred in the interim? Even if these earlier bombings were unsuccessful, and no one was not willing to take the next step and introduce ground forces, what would be the loss in attempting to determine whether this limited use of force would suffice to deter the Serbs from engaging in further aggression? We certainly could not appear any more powerless than we have through our failure since 1991 to put an end to this destructive war between the Serbs, Croats, and Bosnian Muslims.

Now it might be the case that Hoffmann really wants to allow for interventions whenever the UN or regional organizations are "incapable of dealing with . . . an issue."[5] If this is so, it would allow for unilateral intervention in the Yugoslavia situation. Unfortunately, however, the standard Hoffmann employs here would leave the door too widely open for unilateral intervention because there can be good moral reasons why the UN or regional organizations are incapable of dealing with a particular issue. So we don't want to justify unilateral intervention whenever these organizations are incapable of dealing with an issue. I propose, therefore, as a friendly amendment, that we need a norm that says that unilateral intervention can be justified even in the absence of UN or regional approval when the reasons why this approval has been withheld are not morally weighty and, in addition, there is ample evidence that the cause and motives of those who would intervene are morally good.[6]

5. Gaining a Rhetorical Advantage

Throughout his two lectures and in his other work, Stanley Hoffmann is worried about the criticism of moral norms that comes from the doctrine of realism in international relations. The doctrine of realism in international relations is the doctrine that every nation ought to purse its national interest, even at the expense of morality. As it turns out, no one seems to want to be unrealistic in international relations, even if that means qualifying the requirements of morality to some degree.

I want to point out that this use of the term "realism" in international relations differs from the use of the term in recent moral and political philosophy. The term "realism" has been appropriated in moral and political philosophy by those who hold that there are objective moral norms. So in moral and political philosophy, we have moral realists who defend a moral realism of objective moral norms. As a consequence, defenders of objective moral norms have a rhetorical advantage in moral and political philosophy that their counterparts lack in the field of international relations. This suggests that at least some of the difficulty that defenders of moral norms may have in international relations derives from their opponents having gained a rhetorical advantage over them by appropriating the term "realism." Maybe it is time, therefore, for those who defend moral norms in the field of international relations to regain the rhetorical high ground by claiming the term "realism" for themselves. Maybe they could join moral and political philosophers and describe themselves as "moral realists" and cast their opponents as "nonmoral realists" or "immoral realists." It is just a rhetorical trick, but it still might help.

NOTES

1. See Stanley Hoffmann, "Yugoslavia: Implications for Europe and for European Institutions" (forthcoming).

2. Hoffmann, chapter 3, 49. This possibility was actually not suggested in Hoffmann's public lectures. Hoffmann first mentioned it during a subsequent dinner when he was asked when military intervention might have been appropriate.

3. Hoffmann, chapter 2, 22.

4. This objection was suggested to me by Raimo Väyrynen.

5. Hoffmann, chapter 2, 22.

6. In his public response to these comments, Hoffmann accepted this friendly amendment.

6

COMMENTS ON COMMENTS
Stanley Hoffmann

I HAVE NO significant disagreements with Prof. Sterba. As this commentator has indicated, I accept his "friendly amendment." In the Yugoslav tragedy, blame can be spread very widely. Certainly, the various organizations involved—the European Union, the UN, NATO—have often acted lamentably and ineffectively. But fundamentally this was the fault of the main powers, without whose initiatives and support those organizations can only display their own muddles. I would simply like to point out that Prof. Sterba's formulation of the Kantian approach (which he himself describes as the "currently" most favored formulation) is the Rawlsian version of it, and that Kant's own was very different, as Rawls recognized. My own is, if I may say so, more Kantian than Rawlsian, insofar as my emphasis is on a moral sense of duty, and not on a consensus.

Much of what Prof. Johansen proposes is wise and worthy of consideration by statesmen and scholars. There are two points over which I want to argue with him. First, while I agree with him that we need to distinguish cases of collective security against aggression from interventions in a country's internal affairs aimed at protecting human rights, and while I am quite willing to call the latter cases of humanitarian intervention, there *are* instances in which domestic turmoil or domestic policies that do not endanger human rights immediately constitute a threat to regional or world peace—through the production of flows of refugees or because the internal war threatens to spill over into other countries or because, say, a state's nuclear program threatens the stability and security of the area. These cases may well not call for "humanitarian" intervention as it is defined by Prof. Johansen, but intervention may be justified anyhow. The language of Article 2(7) of the Charter, with its intransigent defense of sovereignty, must be read in the light of Chapter VII, which allows the Security Council to take action when there occur threats to peace and security. Moreover, as long as the UN has not firmly established the norm Prof. Johansen and I both advocate—i.e., the validity of intervention for human rights—it is better to have the UN "cover" some of its interventions aimed at protecting these rights by arguing that their violation threatens peace and security (cf. the case of the Kurds in Iraq) than to have the UN default altogether. And I see nothing wrong, on the contrary, in asserting that massive violations of human rights should be treated as ipso facto threats to peace and security. A world in which such violations occur routinely would not be safe very long. In the Yugoslav case, we find ground for (1) collective security, insofar as Serbia (and also Croatia, at times) invaded a state recognized by and a member of the UN, (2) intervention in a civil war that is a threat to regional peace (if only because of the danger of spreading to other parts of the Balkans), and (3) intervention to protect human rights.

My other disagreement with Prof. Johansen concerns his distaste for military intervention. I share many of his reservations about it. Force is a blunt and often counterproductive instrument. And yet it is sometimes—when prevention fails—the only realistic one (in Somalia, sanctions would not have stopped famine). Mohammed Sahnoun may not remember a case in which military intervention by the UN was effective, but I can: in putting an end to Tschombe's secession during the Congo crisis. Moreover, the alternatives preferred by Prof. Johansen have their own flaws. Sanctions work better in the long than in the short run, and in the long run the victims whom humanitarian intervention seeks to rescue may well be dead: sanctions and aerial pinpricks did not save the men of Srebrenica. Holding leaders responsible and prosecuting them for war crimes and crimes against humanity are a moral imperative, and may offer advantages over force and sanctions, but the obstacles to such a course, in a world where criminal leaders are protected by sovereignty and where "realistic" diplomats find doing business with them necessary, remain formidable. Nor is the distinction suggested by Prof. Johansen, between military combat and police enforcement, a very useful one. Police enforcement by an international organization (as opposed to peacekeeping after a cease-fire or an agreement), while it may entail far smaller forces than collective security against an aggressor, is likely to require some resort to force to protect "safe areas," for instance, or to defeat interference with the delivery of humanitarian assistance.

I am grateful to my commentators for their criticisms and thoughtful suggestions. See my "Politics and Ethics of Military Intervention," in *Survival*, Winter 1995–96, vol. 37 no. 4, pp. 29–51, which continues the discussion of the issues of chapters 2 and 3.

APPENDIX
Peacekeeping Operations with Humanitarian
Components since 1990
Prepared by Robert C. Johansen and Kurt Mills

ANGOLA

United Nations Angola Verification Mission (UNAVEM I)
- Duration: January 1989 to June 1991
- Strength: 70 military observers
- Cost: $14.7 million (January 1991)
- Fatalities: None
- Contributors: Algeria, Argentina, Brazil, Congo, Czechoslovakia, India, Jordan, Norway, Spain, Yugoslavia
- Mandate: To verify the withdrawal of Cuban troops from Angola (Resolution 626).
- Assessment: The withdrawal was successfully completed by May 25, 1991, more than a month early. UNAVEM I fully carried out its mandate, although civil war broke out again within Angola.

United Nations Angola Verification Mission II (UNAVEM II)
- Duration: June 1991 to February 1995
- Strength: 350 military observers, 126 police observers, plus 400 electoral observers
- Cost: $26.3 million (1994)
- Fatalities: 4
- Contributors: Argentina, Brazil, Congo, Guinea Bissau, Hungary, India, Jordan, Malaysia, Morocco, Netherlands, New Zealand, Nigeria, Norway, Slovak Republic, Sweden, Zimbabwe
- Mandate: To verify the cease-fire between the government and

UNITA rebels, to create a new joint army, and to monitor the Angolan police until elections were held (Resolution 696). Resolution 747 expanded the mandate to include election monitoring. The number of personnel was reduced, although gradually increased again. Resolutions 785, 793, 804, 834, 851, 864, 890, 903, 922, 932, 945, 952, 966 extended the mandate. The operation became UNAVEM III as the UN prepared to monitor the Lusaka Protocol outlining a new cease-fire.

• Assessment: A peace agreement in mid-1991 appeared to end 16 years of warfare. An estimated 100,000 refugees returned to their homes. National elections held in September 1992 were rated as "generally free and fair" by international observers on the scene. After elections, fighting broke out because the losers (UNITA) refused to accept the outcome. The new round of fighting was more vicious than any time previously in Angola's civil wars, severely limiting the success of the UN operation. Yet imposing a cease-fire was not within the UN's mandate or capability. Humanitarian operations included attempting to provide assistance to as many as 2 million Angolans, although frequently the security situation precluded the delivery of aid.

United Nations Angola Verification Mission (UNAVEM III)
• Duration: February 1995 to present
• Strength: (Authorized) 7,000 troops, plus 350 military observers and 260 police observers
• Cost: Estimated $383 million annually
• Fatalities: None
• Contributors: Bangladesh, Brazil, India, Kenya, Pakistan, United Kingdom, Uruguay, Zimbabwe
• Mandate: The Lusaka Accords of November 20, 1994, called for demobilization of UNITA's troops, an integrated national army, a power-sharing agreement, and the presence of a large UN peacekeeping force to oversee the peace process. Resolution 952 called on the UN to "assist the parties in restoring peace and achieving national reconciliation in Angola," including monitoring the cease-fire and the flow of humanitarian assistance.
• Assessment: After several months of operation the force of

7,000 seemed to be accomplishing its mission, although several major issues remained unresolved.

CAMBODIA

United Nations Advance Mission in Cambodia (UNAMIC)
- Duration: October 1991 to March 1992
- Strength: (Authorized) 50 military liaison officers, 8 civilian liaison staff, 20 other military personnel, 40 person military communications unit, 75 international and 75 local civilian support staff
- Cost: $20 million
- Fatalities: None
- Contributors: Algeria, Argentina, Australia, Austria, Bangladesh, Belgium, Canada, China, France, Germany, Ghana, India, Indonesia, Ireland, Malaysia, Netherlands, New Zealand, Pakistan, Poland, Russian Federation, Senegal, Thailand, Tunisia, United Kingdom, United States, Uruguay
- Mandate: To maintain a cease-fire until UNTAC could be established. UNAMIC was created by Resolution 717 after the signing of the Paris Agreements on a Comprehensive Political Settlement of the Cambodia Conflict. Resolution 728 expanded the mandate to include mine-clearance activities. When UNTAC became operational it absorbed UNAMIC.
- Assessment: This limited UN operation succeeded in preparing the way for the UN Transitional Authority in Cambodia.

United Nations Transitional Authority in Cambodia (UNTAC)
- Duration: March 1992 to September 1993 (Withdrawal completed by November 15, 1993)
- Strength: 22,000
- Cost: $1.6 billion (Total for both UNAMIC and UNTAC)
- Fatalities: 55
- Contributors: Algeria, Argentina, Australia, Austria, Bangladesh, Belgium, Brunei Darussalam, Bulgaria, Cameroon, Canada, Chile, China, Colombia, Egypt, Fiji, France, Germany, Ghana, Hun-

gary, India, Indonesia, Ireland, Italy, Japan, Jordan, Kenya, Malaysia, Morocco, Namibia, Nepal, Netherlands, New Zealand, Nigeria, Norway, Pakistan, Philippines, Poland, Russian Federation, Senegal, Singapore, Sweden, Thailand, Tunisia, United Kingdom, United States, Uruguay

• Mandate: To implement the Paris Agreements, UNTAC was given "all powers necessary" to undertake this mandate (Resolution 745). UNTAC was to supervise government functions, maintain a cease-fire, and administer elections while rebuilding the country, disarming the factions, and facilitating refugee repatriation. The mandate included protecting human rights, supervising the civil police, organizing and conducting free and fair general elections, disarming forces, overseeing government ministries, maintaining law and order, repatriating and resettling Cambodian refugees and displaced persons, and rehabilitating essential Cambodian infrastructure. Other relevant Security Council Resolutions, mostly having to do with the elections and withdrawal, include 766, 783, 792, 826, 835, 840, 860, and 880.

• Assessment: This large, complicated UN operation succeeded in administering a most difficult transition, including an election campaign and vote, and the repatriation of 370,000 refugees from the Thai-Cambodian border. UNTAC was unable to carry out the disarming of all the factions, especially the Khmer Rouge, or assure the protection of human rights. Nonetheless, UNTAC persisted, elections were held in May 1993 and were generally accepted, and the main objectives of the Paris Agreements were fulfilled. Except for a small number of individuals involved with mine clearance, military police, and medical units, all personnel were withdrawn by November 15, 1993. Thereafter the political situation has become more unstable and the institutionalization of democracy remains uncertain.

EL SALVADOR

United Nations Observer Mission in El Salvador (ONUSAL)
• Duration: July 1991 to April 1995
• Strength: (Authorized) 1,000 military and police personnel, 170 international civilian staff, and 187 local staff

- Cost: $29.2 million (1994)
- Fatalities: 3
- Contributors: Argentina, Austria, Brazil, Canada, Chile, Colombia, Ecuador, France, Guyana, India, Ireland, Italy, Mexico, Spain, Sweden, Venezuela
- Mandate: "To monitor all agreements concluded between the Government of El Salvador and the FMLN, and to verify the compliance by the parties with the San José Agreement on Human Rights" (Resolution 693). This involved active monitoring of the human rights situation, investigating individual cases of violations as well as generally promoting human rights, and making recommendations. On 14 January 1992, the mandate was enlarged (Res. 729) to include two new divisions to complement the original human rights division: military and police. The military division's mandate was to verify the cessation of the armed conflict, monitor the troops and resources of both parties in their new peacetime locations, and later to monitor the destruction of arms. The police division monitored and assisted in the creation of the new Salvadoran National Civil Police, and monitored the Auxiliary Transitional Police (PAT) in the transitional period before the National Civil Police were operational. The mandate was expanded again on 27 May 1993 to include observation of the electoral process, a task performed by the electoral division created in September of that year.
- Assessment: Although not all human rights violations were eliminated, the UN operation overall succeeded in carrying out its mandate.

HAITI

United Nations Mission in Haiti (UNMIH)
- Duration: September 1993 to June 1996
- Strength: (Authorized) 6,000 troops, 900 civilian police, 250 international civilian staff, 200 local staff
- Cost: $316 million total
- Fatalities: 6
- Contributors: (Originally) Argentina, Algeria, Austria, Canada,

France, Indonesia, Madagascar, the Russian Federation, Senegal, Spain, Switzerland, Tunisia, Venezuela, and the United States. The advance team (1994): Austria, Bangladesh, Canada, Djibouti, France, Guatemala, Ireland, New Zealand, United States.

• Mandate: To establish and train a new Haitian police force, monitor the police, assist in the conversion of some military facilities to civilian use, renovate medical facilities, and provide a secure environment for democratic elections (Resolution 867). Original strength level was 567 UN police monitors and a 700-person military construction unit. The initial deployment was prevented by armed civilians. Resolutions 905 and 933 extended the mandate. Resolution 940 called on member states to form a multinational force under unified command and "to use all necessary means" to return President Aristide to power. It also extended the mandate and expanded the number of troops to 6,000. Under the terms of 940, the United States, along with other countries, deployed 21,000 troops to ensure the terms of an agreement to return Aristide to power. UNMIH was finally deployed on March 31, 1995, when it replaced the United States force.

• Assessment: After at first totally failing to force the Haitian military government to agree to the peace accords it had previously signed, the second United Nations-endorsed and U.S.-led pressure did succeed in restoring the legitimate government of Aristide to power.

IRAQ

United Nations Iraq-Kuwait Observation Mission (UNIKOM)
• Duration: April 1991 to present
• Strength: (Authorized) 3,645; Current strength: 1,124 military personnel—243 military observers, 881 troops and support personnel—plus 80 international civilian staff and 130 local civilian staff. The force was unarmed.
• Cost: $68.6 million (1994)
• Fatalities: 3

- Contributors: Argentina, Austria, Bangladesh, Canada, China, Denmark, Fiji, Finland, France, Ghana, Greece, Hungary, India, Indonesia, Ireland, Italy, Kenya, Malaysia, Nigeria, Pakistan, Poland, Romania, Russia, Senegal, Singapore, Sweden, Thailand, Turkey, United Kingdom, United States, Uruguay, Venezuela
- Mandate: To monitor a buffer zone between the two countries after the Gulf War. Resolution 689 called for monitoring the DMZ and the Khawr 'Abd Allah waterway between Iraq and Kuwait "to deter violations of the boundary through its presence in, and surveillance of, the demilitarized zone; and to observe any hostile action mounted from the territory of one State against the other." Resolution 806 expanded the mandate to include the ability to take action to prevent or address small violations of the DMZ or boundary. It also increased the number of authorized troops to 3,645.
- Assessment: According to a September 1995 report by the Secretary General, the unarmed mission "continued to contribute significantly to the calm that prevailed in the area of operation." Since Iraq's formal acceptance of the newly demarcated border in November, 1994, the mission has had the cooperation of both Iraqi and Kuwaiti authorities, and only minor violations have been reported.

Northern Iraq

- Duration: April 1991 to present
- Mandate: To protect the Kurdish population in northern Iraq through the establishment of no-fly zones and Kurdish enclaves. A few of the Allied countries that defeated Iraq during the 1991 Gulf War, including the United States, France, and the United Kingdom, initiated this operation. Resolution 688 identified the repression of the Kurds as a threat to international peace and security and called on all member states to contribute to the humanitarian effort. Whereas other resolutions, such as the one authorizing U.S. intervention in Somalia, called on states to use "all necessary means" to address the situation, the mandate in Northern Iraq did not go this far. Thus the legal basis for this operation is less clear. The Allied powers have carried out the spirit more than the letter of Resolution 688.

- Assessment: This operation in practice temporarily created a de facto autonomous Kurdish province in northern Iraq. It protected the Kurds from the Iraqi government's hostility to this minority population, providing security and humanitarian relief. Elections were held in 1992 and a fragile coalition government established, although the territory is in fact divided between two rival Kurdish organizations. The UN presence allowed a Turkish incursion into Iraq, lasting several weeks, aimed at Turkish Kurds operating from Iraqi territory.

MOZAMBIQUE

United Nations Operation in Mozambique (ONUMOZ)
- Duration: December 1992 to January 1995
- Strength: approximately 6,500
- Cost: $294.8 million (1994)
- Fatalities: 17
- Contributors: Argentina, Australia, Austria, Bangladesh, Botswana, Brazil, Canada, Cape Verde, China, Czech Republic, Egypt, Ghana, Guinea Bissau, Guyana, Hungary, India, Indonesia, Italy, Japan, Jordan, Malaysia, Nepal, Netherlands, New Zealand, Nigeria, Pakistan, Portugal, the Russian Federation, Spain, Sri Lanka, Sweden, Togo, United States, Uruguay, Zambia
- Mandate: To implement peace accords between the government and the rebel group RENAMO, monitor the cease-fire, separate and demobilize forces, provide security for selected transportation routes, facilitate refugee repatriation, monitor the elections agreed to in the cease-fire agreement, and coordinate humanitarian assistance (Resolution 797). Various deployments were authorized by Resolutions 782 and 882. Other relevant resolutions include 863, 898, 916.
- Assessment: The UN operation maintained the cease-fire agreement and monitored the electoral campaign and voting in October 1994. This multidimensional mission was widely heralded as successful.

NICARAGUA

United Nations Observer Group in Central America (ONUCA)

- Duration: December 1989 to January 1992
- Strength: 1,098
- Cost: $90.5 million total
- Fatalities: None
- Contributors: Argentina, Brazil, Canada, Colombia, Ecuador, India, Ireland, Spain, Sweden, Venezuela
- Mandate: To monitor compliance with the Esquipulas II peace agreement, demobilize armed forces, monitor political campaigns, and help administer and certify elections.
- Assessment: Despite difficulties in demobilizing forces and stopping all violence, the UN monitors succeeded in helping the peace agreement to hold and the electoral results, although adverse to the ruling Sandinista government, to be accepted by all parties.

RWANDA

United Nations Observer Mission Uganda-Rwanda (UNOMUR)

- Duration: June 1993 to June 1994
- Strength: 81 military observers, 17 international staff, and 7 local personnel
- Cost: Included with UNAMIR below
- Fatalities: None
- Contributors: Bangladesh, Botswana, Brazil, Hungary, Netherlands, Senegal, Slovak Republic, Zimbabwe
- Mandate: To "monitor the Uganda / Rwanda border to verify that no military assistance reaches Rwanda," with the focus being primarily on transport by roads or tracks that "could accommodate vehicles of lethal weapons and ammunition across the border, as well as any other material which could be of military use" (Resolution 846). These actions were intended to decrease tensions between the

Rwandan government and the Rwandese Patriotic Front (RPF). The governments of both Rwanda and Uganda requested this force. Resolutions 891 and 928 extended the mandate.

• Assessment: The UN operation successfully fulfilled its limited monitoring mandate, but later failed to protect tens of thousands of civilians who were massacred.

United Nations Assistance Mission for Rwanda (UNAMIR)
• Duration: October 1993 to March 1996
• Strength: 5,442 military personnel and 80 civilian police
• Cost: Approximately $98 million annually
• Fatalities: 26
• Contributors: Argentina, Australia, Austria, Bangladesh, Canada, Chad, Congo, Djibouti, Ethiopia, Fiji, Ghana, Guinea, Guinea Bissau, India, Jordan, Malawi, Mali, Niger, Nigeria, Poland, the Russian Federation, Senegal, Tunisia, United Kingdom, Uruguay, Zambia, Zimbabwe
• Mandate: "(a) To contribute to the security of the city of Kigali, inter alia, within a weapons secure area established by the parties in and around the city; (b) To monitor observance of the cease-fire agreement, which calls for the establishment of cantonment and assembly zones and the demarcation of the new demilitarized zone and other demilitarization procedures; (c) To monitor the security situation during the final period of the transitional government's mandate, leading up to the elections; (d) To assist with mine clearance, primarily through training programmes; (e) To investigate at the request of the parties or on its own initiative instances of alleged non-compliance with the provisions of the Arusha Peace Agreement relating to the integration of the armed forces, and pursue any such instances with the parties responsible and report thereon as appropriate to the Secretary General; (f) To monitor the process of repatriation of Rwandese refugees and resettlement of displaced persons to verify that it is carried out in a safe and orderly manner; (g) To assist in the coordination of humanitarian assistance activities in conjunction with relief operations; (h) To investigate and report on incidents regarding the activities of the gendarmerie and police" (Resolution 872). The initial authorized troop strength

was 2,548. Resolutions 891 and 909 extended the mandate. After the inter-ethnic massacres and civil war erupted in April 1994, Resolution 912 reduced the number of troops to 270 and changed the mandate to act as an intermediary between the government and rebel forces, assist in humanitarian relief operations where possible, and monitor the situation. Resolution 918 expanded the mandate to include protection of refugees and civilians through the creation of secure humanitarian areas and to provide security for relief operations. It also expanded the number of troops to 5,500. Resolution 929 authorized member states to use "all necessary means" to carry out humanitarian operations, opening the way for the French initiative, which focused on creating a "humanitarian protected zone" in southwestern Rwanda. Resolution 965 extended the mandate and expanded it to include protection of the international war crimes tribunal for Rwanda and human rights officers, as well as to help train a new police force.

- Assessment: The UN force fulfilled its initial monitoring functions quite well, but clearly it lacked authority and the means to promote social integration. When massive genocide occurred in April 1994, the UN forces were ineffective in protecting victims from widespread slaughter. The UN presence was highly successful in organizing and providing relief to millions of refugees and displaced persons. Still, the UN and its members gave insufficient attention to reconstructing the country and helping refugees and displaced persons to return safely to their homes.

SOMALIA

United Nations Operation in Somalia I (UNOSOM I)
- Duration: April 1992 to April 1993
- Strength: (Authorized) 4,219
- Cost: $109.7 million
- Fatalities: None
- Contributors: Australia, Austria, Bangladesh, Belgium, Canada, Czechoslovakia, Egypt, Fiji, Finland, Indonesia, Jordan, Morocco, New Zealand, Norway, Pakistan, Zimbabwe

• Mandate: To monitor the cease-fire in Mogadishu, provide security for UN personnel, equipment, and supplies, and escort humanitarian supply distribution in and near the city (Resolution 751). Resolution 775 expanded the number of troops to 4,219. Resolution 794 authorized the use of "all necessary means to establish as soon as possible a secure environment for humanitarian relief operations in Somalia," and provided the basis for the U.S.-led deployment of the Unified Task Force (UNITAF) on December 9, 1992, which, at its height, involved 37,000 troops.

• Assessment: This portion of UN and U.S. involvement proved quite successful in securing the administration of food aid to severely malnourished people, saving as many as 350,000 to 500,000 lives.

United Nations Operation in Somalia II (UNOSOM II)
• Duration: May 1993 to March 1995
• Strength: (Authorized) 28,000 troops plus 2,800 civilian staff; also 17,700 troops in the U.S. Joint Task Force in Somalia not under UN operational command
• Cost: $862.2 million (1994)
• Fatalities: 134
• Contributors: Australia, Bangladesh, Egypt, Ghana, India, Indonesia, Ireland, Italy, Malaysia, Nepal, Netherlands, Nigeria, Pakistan, Philippines, Republic of Korea, Zambia, Zimbabwe
• Mandate: To monitor and maintain a cessation of fighting, control heavy weapons, disarm unauthorized armed groups, protect UN and relief agency personnel, repatriate refugees, and supervise the accord calling for democratic government. Difficulties arose because of the tension, often unrecognized, between the narrow mission to feed the hungry and the broader mission to achieve peace and disarm militarily powerful clan leaders who generated the famine. This tension encouraged "mission creep" on the ground. Resolution 814 created UNOSOM II as a transition from UNITAF and UNOSOM I. Resolution 837 reiterated the mission of UNOSOM II, and led to a more active stance against certain factions. Resolutions 878 and 886 extended the mandate. Resolution 897 extended UNOSOM II, revised its mandate somewhat, and reduced troop

levels to 22,000. The revised mandate included disarmament, protecting ports and airports, providing humanitarian relief, aiding the repatriation effort, and assisting in the political process. Resolutions 946 and 954 further extended the mandate. Resolution 954 set March 31, 1995 as the deadline for the withdrawal of UNOSOM II. The last UN peacekeepers left on March 16, 1995.

• Assessment: UNOSOM II made significant contributions to the humanitarian relief effort but failed to disarm the warring clans and achieve peace. Many observers conclude that the difficulties and failings of UN operations in Somalia were due to failures of leadership among both the heads of government of the permanent members of the Security Council and the Secretary General's office. The great powers did not respond until far too late and then they provided far too few resources to enable the UN to fulfill humanitarian assistance at minimum cost. The use of force by U.S. military personnel and the subsequent loss of life led to a U.S. decision to withdraw. This bad experience also undermined support in the U.S. public and Congress for participating in UN operations. By the time UNOSOM left Somalia, there was no political solution in sight, and sporadic fighting continued.

YUGOSLAVIA AND SUCCESSOR STATES

United Nations Protection Force (UNPROFOR)
• Duration: March 1992 to December 1995
• Strength: 22,419 (June 1995); 39,789 (December 1994)
• Cost: Approximately $1.9 billion annually
• Fatalities: 167
• Contributors: Argentina, Bangladesh, Belgium, Brazil, Canada, Colombia, Czech Republic, Denmark, Egypt, Finland, France, Ghana, Indonesia, Ireland, Jordan, Kenya, Lithuania, Malaysia, Nepal, Netherlands, New Zealand, Nigeria, Norway, Pakistan, Poland, Portugal, Russia, Slovak Republic, Spain, Sweden, Switzerland, Tunisia, Turkey, Ukraine, United Kingdom, United States, Venezuela
• Mandate: To "create the conditions of peace and security required for the negotiation of an overall settlement of the Yugoslav

crisis" (Resolution 743). The original mandate was for one year and focused on demilitarization of UN Protected Areas, mainly in Croatia. In Croatia the mandate included ensuring the demilitarization of protected areas, monitoring police activities, and verifying the withdrawal of Yugoslav armed forces. In Bosnia the mandate used Chapter VII as its basis and called on states and regional organizations to protect humanitarian convoys (Resolution 770). Resolution 776 officially gave that duty to UNPROFOR. Resolution 781 asked UNPROFOR to monitor a ban on military flights in Bosnia-Herzegovina. In Macedonia, the mandate included monitoring border areas to deter attacks by Serbs or others. Resolution 795 drew upon Chapter VIII and a request by Macedonia to deploy the UN's first preventive force to prevent the spread of fighting into that country. Resolutions 807, 815, 847, and 871 extended the period of the mandate. Resolution 816 expanded the ban on military flights and, relying on Chapter VII, authorized member states to take action to enforce the ban. Resolutions 819 and 824 created "Safe Areas" in Bosnia-Herzegovina that were to be free from hostilities. Resolution 836 expanded the mandate to enable UNPROFOR to take military action to ensure the protection of the Safe Areas. Resolution 844 expanded UNPROFOR by 7,600 troops. Resolution 908 extended the mandate until September 30, 1994 and increased the size of the force by another 3,500 troops. Resolution 914 increased this, again, by 6,550 troops, 150 military observers, and 275 civilian police monitors. Resolution 958 extended to Croatia the authorization provided in 836 to use military means to protect Safe Areas. Dozens of other resolutions condemned actions taken by the parties, extended mandates to include border control, and reiterated previous resolutions. On March 31, 1995, UNPROFOR was divided into three separate missions. UNPROFOR continued to operate in Bosnia-Herzegovina. UNCRO took over the activities of UNPROFOR in Croatia (see UNCRO), and UNPREDEP continued operations in Macedonia. In August and September 1994, the UN authorized air strikes by NATO on Serbian heavy gun emplacements used to shell civilian areas.

• Assessment: The preventive deployment in Macedonia succeeded in preventing the spread of fighting to that region. However, UN operations in Croatia and Bosnia failed to prevent ethnic "cleansing," the continuation of fighting in Bosnia and Croatia, repeated shelling of civilians, and attacks on and over-running of "UN-protected safe areas." The successful Serbian attacks on Srebrenica and Zepa in 1995 contributed to the subsequent decision to use NATO air-strikes against Serbian shelling of Sarajevo and elsewhere. UNPROFOR also failed to dissuade Croatia from using force to re-capture Western Slavonia and other territory from Serbia in 1995. Nonetheless, despite many failures and UN personnel even being taken hostage, the UN presence mitigated the extent and degree of violence in Sarajevo and some other areas. The humanitarian assistance no doubt enabled many to survive who otherwise would have died, but even these successes were limited by the frequent closure of the Sarajevo airport and blocking of transportation routes by the Bosnian Serbs.

United Nations Confidence Restoration Operation in Croatia (UNCRO)
- Duration: March 1995 to January 1996
- Strength: 14,423 (June 1995)
- Cost: Included with UNPROFOR above
- Fatalities: 16
- Contributors: Argentina, Belgium, Canada, Czech Republic, Denmark, Estonia, France, Indonesia, Jordan, Kenya, Lithuania, Nepal, Netherlands, Norway, Poland, Russia, Slovak Republic, Sweden, Ukraine, United States
- Mandate: To continue the work of UNPROFOR in Croatia under a different structure (Resolutions 981 and 990).
- Assessment: UNCRO helped to implement a cease-fire between government and Serb forces, to control the movement of military equipment and personnel across borders, to facilitate the delivery of humanitarian assistance into Bosnia-Herzegovina, and to implement all other relevant resolutions.

United Nations Preventive Deployment Force (UNPREDEP)
- Duration: April 1995 to present
- Strength: 1,044 (June 1995)
- Cost: Included with UNPROFOR above

- Fatalities: None
- Contributors: Denmark, Finland, Sweden, United States
- Mandate: To continue the work of UNPROFOR in Macedonia under a separate structure (Resolution 983).
- Assessment: It succeeded in discouraging the outbreak of fighting in Macedonia, in part because it (1) prevented the expansion of Serbia to Macedonia, probably because Belgrade did not want to challenge the force enjoying U.S. support and containing U.S. personnel, and (2) stabilized internal conditions and inter-ethnic relations in Macedonia.